First World War
and Army of Occupation
War Diary
France, Belgium and Germany

38 DIVISION
113 Infantry Brigade
Royal Welsh Fusiliers
16th Battalion
2 December 1915 - 27 April 1919

WO95/2556/2

The Naval & Military Press Ltd
www.nmarchive.com
Published in association with The National Archives

Published by

The Naval & Military Press Ltd

Unit 10 Ridgewood Industrial Park,

Uckfield, East Sussex,

TN22 5QE England

Tel: +44 (0) 1825 749494

www.naval-military-press.com

www.nmarchive.com

This diary has been reprinted in facsimile from the original. Any imperfections are inevitably reproduced and the quality may fall short of modern type and cartographic standards.

© Crown Copyright
Images reproduced by permission of The National Archives, London, England, 2015.

Contents

Document type	Place/Title	Date From	Date To
Heading	WO95/2556/2		
Heading	16th Bn Roy. Welsh Fus. Dec 1915-Apr 1919		
Heading	38th Div 16th R.W. Fus. Vol I December 1915		
War Diary	Winchester	02/12/1915	04/12/1915
War Diary	Boulogne	04/12/1915	10/12/1915
War Diary	Laventie	10/12/1915	18/12/1915
War Diary	Mametz	19/12/1915	19/12/1915
War Diary	Batt HQ K27 B. 3.9	20/12/1915	31/12/1915
Heading	16th R.W. Fus. Vol 2 January 1916		
War Diary	Battn HQ K 27. B 39 Ref Map. 36. A	01/01/1916	06/01/1916
War Diary	Bn H Q. S.9. A 6.5	06/01/1916	07/01/1916
War Diary	Bn H Q. S.9. A 6.5 Ref 36 SW Sheet 3	08/01/1916	10/01/1916
War Diary	Richebourg St Vaast	11/01/1916	14/01/1916
War Diary	Vielle Chapelle	15/01/1916	23/01/1916
War Diary	Battn HQ S. 9 A 6.5 Ref. Map 36 SW Sheet 3	24/01/1916	27/01/1916
War Diary	Richebourg-St Vaast	28/01/1916	31/01/1916
Map			
Heading	Diary 16th R. Welsh Fusiliers (113th Inf Bde. 38th Divn) Feb 1916		
War Diary	Bn HQ At M. S 9 A 5.5 Ref. Map 36 Sub Sheet Trenches Map	01/02/1916	04/02/1916
War Diary	Richebourg St Vaast	05/02/1916	08/02/1916
War Diary	Vielle Chapelle	08/02/1916	16/02/1916
War Diary	Givenchy	17/02/1916	21/02/1916
War Diary	Gorre Map Ref F 3.6 Central Bethune Combined Sheet 5	22/02/1916	25/02/1916
War Diary	Givenchy	26/02/1916	29/02/1916
Heading	16 R. Wesh Fus Vol 4 March 1916		
War Diary	Bn H.Q. Lt A 14 A 9.6 (Brigade Trench Map Area F)	01/03/1916	03/03/1916
War Diary	Bn H.Q. A.8.c.2.3 (Brigade Trench Map Area F)	04/03/1916	08/03/1916
War Diary	Bn H.Q. W. 4.c. 4.6 (Bethune Combined Sheet Ed.6)	09/03/1916	15/03/1916
War Diary	Bn H.Q. At. X.1d 6.2 (Bethune Camp St Ed 6)	17/03/1916	20/03/1916
War Diary	Bn H.Q A.2. B 2.6 Brigade Trench Map Area G	20/03/1916	24/03/1916
War Diary	Bn HQ (S 13.c.1/2 1)	25/03/1916	27/03/1916
War Diary	Bn HQ A 2. B 3.8	28/03/1916	31/03/1916
War Diary	La Pannerie	01/04/1916	08/04/1916
War Diary	Gorre	09/04/1916	17/04/1916
War Diary	HQ At Lt M 34.b 5.9 1/2	17/04/1916	19/04/1916
War Diary	Riez Bailleul	20/04/1916	23/04/1916
War Diary	Merville	24/04/1916	29/04/1916
War Diary	Laventie	30/04/1916	31/05/1916
War Diary	Moated Grange	01/06/1916	15/06/1916
War Diary	Ostreville	16/06/1916	30/06/1916
War Diary	Casualties	30/06/1916	30/06/1916
Heading	16th Battn. The Royal Welsh Fusiliers. July 1916		
Heading	War Diary For July 1916 16 Batt. R.W.F.		
War Diary		01/07/1916	19/07/1916
War Diary	Mailly Maillet	20/07/1916	31/07/1916
Miscellaneous	Appendix I. (Report On Operation In Mametz Wood.)		
Miscellaneous	Appendix I. Operation In Mametz Wood		

Heading	16 Battn. R W F War Diary For August 1916 Vol 9		
War Diary		01/08/1916	31/08/1916
Heading	War Diary 16th Battalion R.W.F. For September 1916		
War Diary		01/09/1916	30/09/1916
Heading	War Diary 16th Batt. Royal Welsh Fusiliers. October 1916		
War Diary	Left Subsector	01/10/1916	15/10/1916
War Diary	Right Sub Sector	15/10/1916	19/10/1916
War Diary	Camp 'P'	20/10/1916	20/10/1916
War Diary	Left Subsector	25/10/1916	30/10/1916
Miscellaneous	Report On Raid Made By 16th Royal Welsh Fusiliers		
Miscellaneous	Report On Raid Carried Out By 16th Battn. R.W. Fusiliers On Night 29/30th Oct. 1916	30/10/1916	30/10/1916
Miscellaneous	38th Div GS 77	30/10/1916	30/10/1916
Heading	War Diary For November 1916 16th Battalion Royal Welsh Fusiliers Vol 12		
War Diary		01/11/1916	30/11/1916
Heading	16th Battn. Royal Welsh Fusiliers. War Diary For December 1916		
War Diary	Left Subsector	01/12/1916	31/12/1916
Heading	War Diary For January 1917 16th Batt. Royal Welsh Fusiliers.		
War Diary		01/01/1917	30/01/1917
Heading	War Diary 16th Battn. R.W.F. February 1917		
War Diary		01/02/1917	28/02/1917
Heading	16th Battn. Royal Welsh Fusiliers War Diary For March 1917		
War Diary	Left Subsector	01/03/1917	01/04/1917
Heading	16th Battn. Royal Welsh Fusiliers. War Diary For April 1917		
War Diary	Left Sub. Sector	01/04/1917	01/05/1917
Heading	16th Royal Welsh Fusiliers. War Diary For May 1917		
War Diary	Right Sub Sector (L'Shire Farm)	01/05/1917	30/05/1917
Heading	16th Batt Royal Welsh Fusiliers. War Diary For June 1917		
War Diary		01/06/1917	30/06/1917
Heading	16th Bn Royal Welsh Fusiliers War Diary July-1917		
War Diary	Rely	01/07/1917	31/07/1917
Miscellaneous	16th Battn. R.W. Fusiliers.	07/08/1917	07/08/1917
Heading	16th Battn Royal Welsh Fusiliers. War Diary August 1917		
War Diary		01/08/1917	31/08/1917
Heading	16th Battn. Royal Welsh Fusiliers. War Diary For September 1917 Vol 22		
War Diary		01/09/1917	30/09/1917
Heading	16th Batt Royal Welsh Fusiliers War Diary For October 1917		
War Diary		01/10/1917	31/10/1917
Heading	16th Batt Royal Welsh Fusiliers War Diary For November 1917 Vol 24		
War Diary		01/11/1917	30/11/1917
Miscellaneous	16th Batt R.W. Fusiliers.	08/11/1917	08/11/1917
Heading	16th Batt. Royal Welsh Fusiliers. War Diary For December 1917		
War Diary	Bois Grenier Left Sector	01/12/1917	03/12/1917
War Diary	Reserve	04/12/1917	07/12/1917

War Diary	Left Subsection Bois Grenier		07/12/1917	11/12/1917
War Diary	Support Area		12/12/1917	15/12/1917
War Diary	Left Subsection Bois Grenier		16/12/1917	17/12/1917
War Diary	Bois Grenier		18/12/1917	20/12/1917
War Diary	Fleurbaix Reserve		21/12/1917	26/12/1917
War Diary	Right Subsection Fleurbaix		27/12/1917	31/12/1917
Heading	16th Batt. Royal Welsh Fusiliers War Diary For January 1918			
War Diary			01/01/1918	31/01/1918
Heading	War Diary 16th Battn. Royal Welsh Fusiliers February 1918			
War Diary			01/02/1918	28/02/1918
Heading	16th Bn. Royal Welsh Fusiliers War Diary For March 1918			
War Diary			01/03/1918	31/03/1918
Heading	16th Battn. The Royal Welsh Fusiliers. April 1918			
Heading	16th Battalion R W Fusrs War Diary April 1918 Vol 29			
War Diary			01/04/1918	30/04/1918
Heading	War Diary For Month Of May 1918 16 R.W.F. Vol 30			
War Diary			01/05/1918	31/05/1918
Heading	16th Batt. Royal Welsh Fusiliers War Diary For June 1918			
War Diary			01/06/1918	30/06/1918
Heading	16th Battn. Royal Welsh Fusiliers. War Diary For July 1918			
War Diary			01/07/1918	31/07/1918
Heading	16th Batt Royal Welsh Fusiliers War Diary For August 1918 Vol 33			
War Diary			01/08/1918	31/08/1918
Heading	War Diary For September 1918 16th Battn. Royal Welsh Fusiliers. Vol 34			
War Diary			01/09/1918	30/09/1918
Heading	16th R W F War Diary For October 1918			
War Diary	Field		01/10/1918	31/10/1918
Heading	16th R.W.F. War Diary For November 1918			
War Diary	Field		01/11/1918	30/11/1918
Heading	16th R.W.F. War Diary For December 1918 Vol 37			
War Diary			01/12/1918	31/12/1918
Heading	16th Bn. Royal Welsh Fusiliers War Diary For January-1919			
War Diary	Field		01/01/1919	29/01/1919
War Diary	Warloy-Baillon		01/02/1919	28/02/1919
War Diary			02/02/1919	22/02/1919
War Diary	Warloy-Baillon		26/02/1919	28/02/1919
War Diary	Warloy-Baillon		12/02/1919	20/02/1919
War Diary	Warloy-Baillon		06/02/1919	06/02/1919
War Diary	Warloy-Baillon		01/03/1919	07/03/1919
War Diary	Blangy-Tronville		18/03/1919	31/03/1919
War Diary	Blangy-Tronville		01/03/1919	27/04/1919

N005/2556/2

38TH DIVISION
113TH INFY BDE

16TH BN ROY. WELCH FUS.
DEC 1915 – APR 1919

16ᵗʰ R.W. Fus:
1st ―
December 1915

121/7936

W.D.   1.F.

Army Form C. 2118.

WAR DIARY
or
INTELLIGENCE SUMMARY.

(Erase heading not required.)

Instructions regarding War Diaries and Intelligence Summaries are contained in F.S. Regs., Part II. and the Staff Manual respectively. Title pages will be prepared in manuscript.

Place	Date	Hour	Summary of Events and Information	Remarks and references to Appendices
Winchester	2/2/15	6.30AM	An advance party strength 3 officers 103 other ranks & all regimental transport proceeded to SOUTHAMPTON by road to embark for active service in FRANCE.	Bty
"	K 2/2/15 4	1 AM	The Battalion and Headquarters entrained in two trains strength 25 Officers & 892 other ranks.	Bty
"	"	6.30AM	Arrived FOLKESTONE and proceeded to embark for FRANCE on active service. Lance Cpl G Currie No17858 detained in hospital at FOLKESTONE.	
BOULOGNE	"	11.45PM	Disembarked at BOULOGNE & marched to rest camp at OSTERHOVE.	
"	5th	8.30AM	Entrained for AIRE	
"	"	1.30PM	Detrained at AIRE and marched to Billets at MAMETZ G 29 C (Ref. map 36A 2nd Edition) and there joined advance party of the Battalion and Transport. The Officer i/c the advance party reported two men Pte Shone 24137 & Pte S E Edwards 18847 missing. These men fell out of have truck with one heavy horse. Remained in Billets until 10th inst.	Bty
"	10th	7.30AM	Battalion, 950 all ranks moved in motor Buses to LAVENTIE M 4 D (ref 36 SW 3rd ED.) The Battalion was here attached for instruction to the 1st Guards Brigade holding front line from N 8.C.5.5. to M 24 D 5.5. approximately (Ref. map 36 S.W. 3rd Ed.) The Battalion was attached in the following manner. A Coy under Capt H H PAINE to 2nd Grenadier Guards. B Coy " Major T R H RICKELLAN - 2nd COLDSTREAM " C Coy " Capt J H FLETCHER - 3rd " D Coy " Capt S L HUNKIN 1st IRISH GUARDS	Bty

WAR DIARY
or
INTELLIGENCE SUMMARY.
(Erase heading not required.)

Army Form C. 2118.

Place	Date	Hour	Summary of Events and Information	Remarks and references to Appendices
LAVENTIE	10/12/15		Each Platoon of this Battalion was attached to a Company of the Guards, and each man was instructed in Sentry during ere by a Guardsman detailed to look after him.	B/g
"	11/12/15		A Coy and C Coy proceeded direct to front line trenches. B Coy and D Coy went No trenches. A Coy " C Coy came out of trenches. Conditions were normal & front very quiet during the 12 hours within is nothing to report. A Coy was killed by a shell while working on a communication trench. and Pte ACoy were wounded by the same shell.	B/g
"	15/12/15		B & D Coy were relieved, and A & C Coys went into trenches. There was nothing to report during 48 hours. Pte was wounded.	B/g
"	16/12/15		A & C Coy were relieved. B & D Coy went into trenches. Nothing to report.	B/g
"	17/12/15		B & D Coy were relieved. A Coy went into LAVENTIE EAST POST & C Coy into trenches. Pte Jones. No by killed while on Sentry duty in front line trenches.	B/g
"	18/12/15		C Coy came out of trenches. A Coy after acting as a fatigue party for the transport of gas cylinders were relieved from LAVENTIE EAST POST.	B/g
"		12.30pm	The Battalion marched out of LAVENTIE & were taken in motor Lorries back to Billets at MAMETZ.	B/g
MAMETZ	19/12/15		Orders received that Battalion is to move at 9.30AM with remainder of 38 Division to new Billeting area at K 21 & 22. (Ref map 36A.)	B/g

Army Form C. 2118.

WAR DIARY
or
INTELLIGENCE SUMMARY.
(Erase heading not required.)

Instructions regarding War Diaries and Intelligence Summaries are contained in F.S. Regs., Part II and the Staff Manual respectively. Title pages will be prepared in manuscript.

Place	Date	Hour	Summary of Events and Information	Remarks and references to Appendices
Batt HQ K27 B39.	26/12/15	3.30p	Battalion marched into Billetting Area. Nothing to report during march. 1 man only fell out and taken to field ambulance.	
"	27/12/15		New Billets area K21 B&D K22 A B&C K27 B&D K28 A&C = Batt HQ at K27 B 5.9. Battalion training commences.	
"	28/12/15		Resting in Billets	
	29			
	30			
	31			

R. M. Carter Lt Col
C.O. 16th Rest
31/12/15

16th R.W. Fus.
Vol 2
January 1916.

WAR DIARY or INTELLIGENCE SUMMARY

Army Form C. 2118.

16. Battalion. R.W.F. January

Place	Date	Hour	Summary of Events and Information	Remarks and references to Appendices
Battn. HQ K29.B39 Ref. Map. 36.A	1st	—	In Billets – Training	
	2nd	—	"	
	3rd		A party consisting of C.O., Adj., Coy Commanders, Coy Sgt Majors left Billets in motor lorries to visit the line held by the 58th Bde. The party visited the front line on night of 3rd & 4th & returned to Billets at 4th.	
	4th		A party consisting of 2nd in Command, 2nd in Command of Coys, NCO per each Coy, Bombing officer, Signalling officer, M.G. officer, Sniping officer visited 58th Bde but did not go into the Trenches.	
	5th		The whole Battalion marched out about 980 strong to take up Billets in Richebourg St Vaast the reserve Brigade Area of the 58th Bde.	
	6th		The whole Battalion moved out of billets and relieved the 6th Battalion Kings from in the front line trenches our dispositions being as follows:— B.Coy (Major McClellan) H. S.10.c.86 to front S.9.D.90 held by 3 platoons with a machine gun on both flanks. One platoon was in Reserve - twenty men & one officer in Capes Keep, the remainder in GUARDSTRENCH. S.10.c.39. "A"+"B" Coys was in a very bad state & impassable. Front S.9.D.90 and Mr S.15.B.9.6½ The Rangers trench connecting trees held by "A"+"B" Coys 6½ "A" Coy (Capt Payne) from front S.15.B.9.6½ to front S.15.D.96. This line was held by 2 platoons. One platoon held BOAR'S HEAD which consists of 4 small isolated posts. One of which includes a Bombers Post. A section was placed in each post. They were isolated during daylight. One platoon held Farm Corner.	see Appendix I

WAR DIARY
or
INTELLIGENCE SUMMARY.

Army Form C. 2118.

1st Battalion R.W.F. January

Place	Date	Hour	Summary of Events and Information	Remarks and references to Appendices
Br Hd S.O.A.43.	6th		The remaining 2 platoons were held in reserve at PALL MALL KEEP, pt. S.15.B.5.d. "C" + "D" Coys were in Reserve. "C" Coy (Capt. Fletcher). Headquarters was at FACTORY CORNER, pt. S.9.D.2+4. 1 Platoon was kept there. They garrisoned CATS POST, pt. S.15.A.7.6, DOGS POST S.9.C.2.9½., ALBERT POST, pt. S.8.D.43., with ten men in each post. 1 Platoon was placed in VINE ST. support trench pt.S.10.C.4.8. o 1st Platoon was posted in FACTORY POST, pt. S.9.D.32. "D" Coy (Capt. Hunkin) Headquarters at No.4 REST HOUSE, pt. S.8.C.46. They garrisoned HEN'S POST + EDWARDS POST with 20 men in each. The remainder of the company was kept at the No.4 REST HOUSE.	See Appendix I
	7th		The relief was carried out without loss, and in good time. During the night of the 6th-7th, fatigue parties for the Front Line were supplied by "C" + "D" Coys. Our Artillery cut enemy wire in front of our line at point, S.10.C.81. Enemy artillery retaliated on our front line & 3 men were wounded in "B" Co. An officer's patrol went out during the night of the 7th-8th to examine wire and not more wire in a very bad state. Our machine guns fired at intervals during the night on gap in enemy's wire. Enemy snipers were very busy at 3 ARM CORNER, but had no victims. Fatigue parties were supplied by the Reserve Coys. Casualties 3330/8 R.F. Day. "B" Co. All wounded. 31456 L. Day. 18845 J. Wilson	
	8th		Very quiet. An observation post was made in the disused trench at point S.15.B.9.9.5 received by 4 snipers.	

16th Battalion R.W.F. January

WAR DIARY
or
INTELLIGENCE SUMMARY.

Army Form C. 2118.

Place	Date	Hour	Summary of Events and Information	Remarks and references to Appendices
Bn H.Qrs. Sq. A.6.5. Ref. 36.S.W. Sheet 3	8th		Reserve Coys supplied the usual fatigue parties in the night. Casualties – Nil.	
	9th		Our artillery shelled enemy wire at S.16.A.5.8. Enemy artillery retaliated on our front line & 2 men were killed & wounded. An officers patrol went out after dark but could find no gap in enemy wire. The usual fatigue parties were supplied at night. Casualties 9/38 L/Cpl W. Jones } "B" Co. Killed 19137 Pte G.A. Thomas } 18615 Sgt J. Matthews 19813 Cpl J. Hodgkinson 12660 L/C R. Pritchard 31419 Pte I.E. Hughes 10896 Pte L.E. Llwellyn 18838 Pte J. Rowlands 23255 Pte J. Davies 23146 Pte W.J. Edmunds	"B" Co wounded
	10th		Non quiet. Casualties:– 19842 Pte H. Humphrys "A" Co. killed by a Ricochet bullet at BOARS HEAD 2nd Lieut. T. Thomas "A" Co killed by a sniper at FARM CORNER. The Battalion was relieved by the 15th Bn R.W.F. and returned to Billets in the Brigade Reserve area at RICHEBOURGH St. VAAST.	
RICHEBOURG –ST VAAST	11th		The Battalion had to evacuate billets 3 times owing to heavy bombardment. A fatigue party of men was supplied by the Battalion to work from 5pm till 11 pm	"
	12th		"	"
	13th		Casualties:– 3 wounded:– 18217 L/Cpl O. Williams "A" Co; 18308 Pte B. Jones; 18493 Pte Y.H. Fleet "D" Co	"

1/6 Battalion R.W.F. January.

WAR DIARY
or
INTELLIGENCE SUMMARY.

Army Form C. 2118.

Place	Date	Hour	Summary of Events and Information	Remarks and references to Appendices
RICHEBOURG H - ST VAAST.	14th	5.30pm	The whole Battalion left RICHEBOURGH-ST VAAST and went into the divisional reserve area of the 19th division at VIEILLE CHAPELLE.	
VIEILLE CHAPELLE	15th		In Billets - cleaning up.	
	16th		" " " "	
	17th		" " Training.	
	18th		" " "	
	19th		" " "	
	20th		" " "	
	21		" " "	
	22		" " "	
	23		The whole Battalion left the divisional Reserve Area at VIEILLE CHAPELLE for the front line trenches and relieved the 9th Battn Cheshire Regt of the 58th Inf Bde. The relief was carried out by 9.10 p.m. Dispositions being as follows:- Two platoons were in the front line, one being at FARM CORNER and "D" Co (Capt. HUNKIN). Two platoons were in Reserve at PALL MALL KEEP the other at BOARS HEAD. The remaining two platoons were in Reserve at PALL MALL KEEP and the OLD BRITISH LINE. "C" Co (Capt. FLETCHER). Three platoons held the front line from COPSE STREET to the RANGERS. One platoon was in Reserve at COPSE KEEP and GUARDS TRENCH. "A" & "B" Coys were in Reserve. "A" Co. (Capt. PAINE) was at No 4 REST HOUSE. "B" Co. (Major McLellan). Headquarters was at FACTORY CORNER. They garrisoned FACTORY KEEP,	

1st Battalion R.W.F.

January.

WAR DIARY
INTELLIGENCE SUMMARY.
(Erase heading not required.)

Army Form C. 2118.

Place	Date	Hour	Summary of Events and Information	Remarks and references to Appendices
	23		and CATS POST. held the new BREASTWORK between VINE St. & CATS POST. Lewis Guns were placed at the following points:— S.16.A.3.5; S.15.A.9.6.5; Sq.9.9.1.; S.10.C.4.5; S.10.D.4.8.1 in the front line, and one gun in each of the following:— GUARDS TRENCH S.10.A.40; FACTORY KEEP, & CATS POST. "A" Coy supplied fatigue parties during the night 23rd-24th. Very quiet. No casualties.	
Battn H.Q. S.9.A.6.5. Old Map 36.S.W. Sheet 3.	24.		Usual working party supplied to R.E. Casualties:— 1 Killed 23802 Pte. A. Young "B"Co. 6 wounded 18883 " W. Williams "C" Co. 19512 " T. Jones "C" Co. 18623 " G. Evans "C" Co. 18394 Cpl. L. Davies "C" Co. 23614 Pte. Y. Thomas "C" Co. 23865 " W. Hughes "C" Co.	
	25.		Very quiet. During the morning 1 platoon "A" Co relieved 2 platoons "C" in the front line from VINE ST. to RANGERS. One platoon "B" Co relieved "C" in the front line from "C" Co front line & COPSE KEEP. One platoon of "C" Co remained in GUARDS TRENCH. Two platoons of "B" Co took over front line trench from COPSE ST. to MDLE ST. from the 10th Battn Welsh Regt. Remaining platoon in new in Support Trench & GUARDS TRENCH. Three platoons of "C" Co took over FACTORY CORNER, FACTORY KEEP, CATS POST & BREASTWORK. One platoon "A" Co relieved 1 platoon of "D" Co in BOARS HEAD. Two platoons "A" Co took over PALL MALL KEEP & OLD BRITISH LINE from "D" Co	

1st Battalion R.W.F.   January.

Army Form C. 2118.

WAR DIARY
or
INTELLIGENCE SUMMARY.
(Erase heading not required.)

Place	Date	Hour	Summary of Events and Information	Remarks and references to Appendices
	25.		Two platoons "D" Co returned to No 4. REST HOUSE & one platoon went into GUARDS TRENCH behind "B" Co. One platoon of "D" Co at FARM CORNER was relieved by the 75th Bn R.W.F. and returned to No 4. REST HOUSE. "D" Coy provided a working party during the night.	
	26.		Very quiet. Casualties:- 1 wounded. 18066 Sgt. W. Davies "D" Co. Usual working parties were supplied. Kaiser's birthday. Enemy bombarded our supports paying particular attention to FACTORY CORNER and the RUE DU BOIS. Our artillery retaliated fully on their front line + supports. Casualties:- 23613 Pte. H. Jones "C" Co. 18624 " Dm. Davies "D" wounded. 23846 " + J. McClement "C"	
	27		The 15th Battn R.W.F. relief being completed by 11.0 pm one man was wounded - No 23168 H. Moore "B" Co. The Battalion moved to Brigade Reserve Area in + about RICHEBOURG - St. VAAST. "A" Co. at RICHEBOURG - St. VAAST. "B" Co on road running from S.2.c.3.15 to S.8.a.95.3. "C" Co at points S.8.D.95, and S.8.B.5.13. "D" Co on RUE des BERCEAUX Garrisons were provided for the following posts:- HENS, EDWARD, LANSDOWNE, ALBERT + DOGS	

16th Battn R.I.R. January

WAR DIARY or INTELLIGENCE SUMMARY

Army Form C. 2118.

Place	Date	Hour	Summary of Events and Information	Remarks and references to Appendices
RICHEBOURG-St VAAST.	28		In Brigade Reserve. 1 working party strength 6 platoons was supplied to the R.E⁰. Casualties - nil.	
	29		In Brigade Reserve. Working parties supplied during the day & the night to the R.E⁰. Casualties - nil.	
	30		In Brigade Reserve. Usual working parties supplied Casualties. No. 96 L/C. Harris "B" Co. M.G. Section killed.	
	31		The whole Battalion left RICHEBOURG-St Vaast and relieved the 15th Battn. R.I.R. ? in the front line trenches.	

A.P. Richards Major
16th B⁶ R.W. Fusiliers

Jan 41.

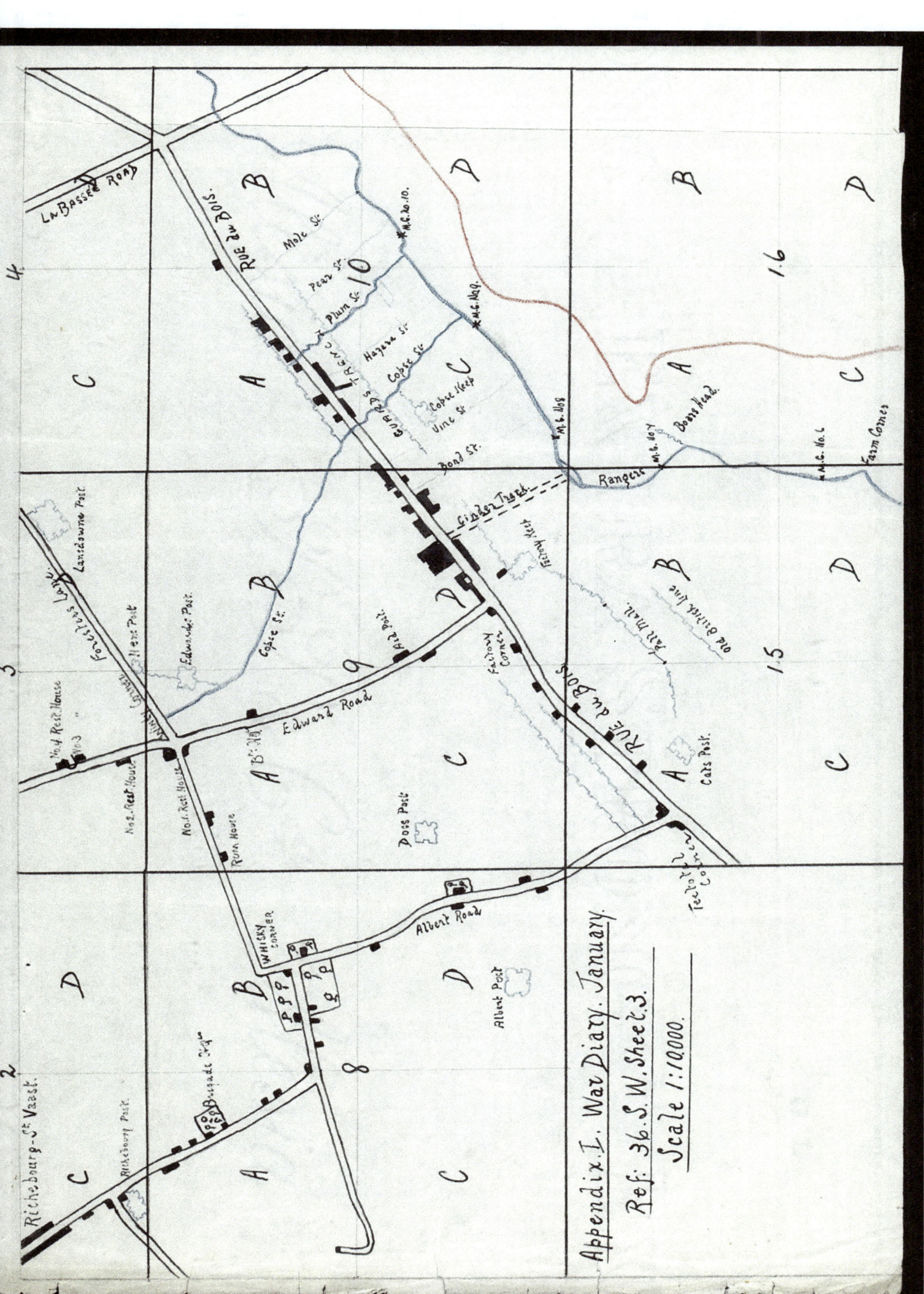

Index

SUBJECT.

No.	Contents.	Date.
	Diary 16th R. Welsh Fusiliers (113th Inf. Bde. 38th Divn) Feb. 1916.	

WAR DIARY or INTELLIGENCE SUMMARY

16th Battn. R.D.F. — February — Army Form C. 2118.

Place	Date	Hour	Summary of Events and Information	Remarks and references to Appendices
Bn. H.Q. at McGATS Ref. Map 36 C.S.W. Sud	1		Our dispositions were as follows:— "D" Coy (Capt. HUNKIN) One platoon in BOAR'S HEAD. Remainder in Reserve in NEW BREASTWORK PALL MALL, STRAND and CATS POST. "C" Coy (Capt. FLETCHER) 2½ platoons in front line between RANGERS and COPSE St. ½ platoon in COPSE KEEP + 1 platoon in GUARDS TRENCH between VINE St – COPSE St. "A" Coy (Capt. PAYNE) 2 platoons in front line between COPSE St + MOLE St. 1 platoon in support trench + 1 platoon in GUARDS TRENCH between COPSE St + PLUM St. "B" Coy (Major McLELLAN) 1 platoon in FACTORY CORNER. Remainder in reserve at NEW REST HOUSE. Very quiet day. An officer's patrol went out during the night. Working party supplied by "B" Co. Ration party supplied by 15th R. Welsh Fus. Casualties – 2/5th L. Whm. 2361 Spottiswood 2 yrs 17 m.o. 23ss/9 2nd Lieut all for duty remained.	
	2		The enemy trench opposite COPSE St was bombarded by Trench Mortar Batteries and Heavy Artillery. Considerable damage was done + enemy retaliation was very weak, amounting to a few bombs thrown into our front line trench – did no material damage. Wiring working party supplied by "B" Co. during the night. 15th R.W.F. supplied a party to work in our front line during the day. Casualties:– Nil	
	3		4.30 am enemy shelled RUE du BOIS + FACTORY CORNER at 6.30 am they shelled B.H.Qrs – WINDY CORNER Many S.A. shells – no material damage done + our artillery retaliated fully. Our artillery bombarded enemy front line trench in front of COPSE St. Retaliation very	

Army Form C. 2118.

16th Battn R.W.F. February

WAR DIARY
or
INTELLIGENCE SUMMARY.
(Erase heading not required.)

Instructions regarding War Diaries and Intelligence Summaries are contained in F.S. Regs., Part II. and the Staff Manual respectively. Title pages will be prepared in manuscript.

Place	Date	Hour	Summary of Events and Information	Remarks and references to Appendices
Br Sig Sch M.Sqrs	3		Weak and divided in FACTORY CORNER. Usual working parties supplied by 'B' Co 15th R.W.F. Casualties:- 23334 Pte J Williams 19528 " J B Griffiths 18993 " A J Williams (self inflicted) wounded	
Ref Maps 1/40,000 France sheet	4		Weather very troublesome during speech. Relieved by 15th Battn R.W.F. Relief complete at 9.30 pm. Battn moved to Brigade Reserve Area in and about RICHEBOURG-ST VAAST. "B" Co garrisoned the following posts:- LANSDOWNE HENS. EDWARDS + DOGS. Casualties nil	
RICHEBOURG ST VAAST	5		In Brigade Reserve. A day working party & a night working party supplied to R.E. A ration party supplied to the 15th R.W.F. Casualties:- L/Sgt H Jones 19430 wounded	
	6		In Brigade Reserve. Usual working parties & ration party supplied. Casualties: Pte T R Chadwick 19091 wounded	
	7		In Brigade Reserve. ditto Casualties:- 19030 Pte R Cliff killed 28390 T James 19611 Pte S John 18968 L/Sgt Williams } wounded 25351 E Thomas wounded 19190 A Jones wounded	
	8		The whole Battn left RICHEBOURG-ST VAAST and moved into the Divisional Reserve Area at Vieille Chapelle.	

2353 Wt. W234/1454 700,000 5/15 D.D.&L. A.D.S.S./Form/C. 2118.

WAR DIARY or INTELLIGENCE SUMMARY

Army Form C. 2118.

16th Batt. R.W.F. February

Place	Date	Hour	Summary of Events and Information	Remarks and references to Appendices
VIEILLÉ CHAPELLE	8		The following posts were taken over by us from the 10th Batt. Welch Regt. in the CROIX BARBEE + VIEILLÉ CHAPELLE System.	
			By "A" Co. St VAAST M.32 D.2.1 1 officer + 30 O.R.	
			PENIN MARIAGE M.31.D.9.8 "	
			CROIX BARBEE M.26.D.2.0 "	
			RUE DU PUITS M.27.C.1.9 "	
			By "B" Co. LORETTO 1 officer + 30 O.R.	
			By "C" Co. VIEILLÉ CHAPELLE R.28.D.66. "	
			HUITS MAISON R.29.B.28 "	
			FOSSE R.22.A.96 "	
			LA TOMBÉ WILLOT R.36.B.05 "	
			LESTREM Q.18.A.20 "	
			PARADIS R.9.C.5.1 "	
			EPINETTE R.4.C.76 "	
			By "D" Co. EUSTON POST 1 officer + 30 O.R.	
			Remainder of Batt. cleaning up. Casualties.	

16th Battn R.W.F.   February   Army Form C. 2118.

WAR DIARY
or
INTELLIGENCE SUMMARY.
(Erase heading not required.)

Instructions regarding War Diaries and Intelligence Summaries are contained in F.S. Regs., Part II. and the Staff Manual respectively. Title pages will be prepared in manuscript.

Place	Date	Hour	Summary of Events and Information	Remarks and references to Appendices
VIEILLE CHAPELLE	9		In pads. Remainder of Battalion doing Routine work	
	10		"	
	11		"	
	12		Pads relieved by 14th Battn R.W.F.	
	13		Routine work. Eight officers visited the new line at GIVENCHY.	
	14		"	
	15		"	
	16		"	
GIVENCHY	17		The whole Battalion left the Brigade Reserve at VIEILLE CHAPELLE to take over the new line of trenches between HAMILTON TERRACE and FIFE St. from the 23rd Battn Royal Fusiliers (10th Spartans). Relief was completed without loss on the exceptionally good time of 2 hours (6.45 pm to 8.45 pm.) Our distribution was as follows:- POPPY REDOUBT. 1 off + 35 O.R "A" Co. NEW CUT and CALEDONIAN ROAD. 2 off + 76 O.R. "A" Co. SCOTTISH TRENCH. 6 off + 169 O.R "B" Co. Sat (H.I.J.K) 1 off + 39 O.R. M Coys. Bombers 13 O.R In support with A Coy	

16th Battn. Royal Irish Fusiliers

WAR DIARY
or
INTELLIGENCE SUMMARY.

(Erase heading not required.)

February 1916

Army Form C. 2118.

Instructions regarding War Diaries and Intelligence Summaries are contained in F.S. Regs., Part II. and the Staff Manual respectively. Title pages will be prepared in manuscript.

Place	Date	Hour	Summary of Events and Information	Remarks and references to Appendices
GIVENCHY	17.		PRINCE'S ISLAND. 1 Off + 26 O.R. "C" Co.	
			GEORGE ST. 1 Off + 28 O.R. "C" Co.	
			LE PLANTIN 2 Off + 60 O.R. "C" Co.	
			22 O.R. "C" Co. To relieve present at Coy H.Qrs.	
			GROUSE BUTTS 3 Off + 153 O.R. "D" Co.	
			GROUSE BUTTS	
			Night quiet. Enemy threw a few bombs & rifle grenades & we retaliated. One working party was dispersed by a rifle grenade. DEADMANS TRENCH was patrolled.	
			Casualties:- Nil	
	18.		The Heavy Trench Mortar Batty. fired a few rounds from the right of our line. The Germans were due to carry out a relief on the night of the 18th-19th & the Artillery carried out a programme which lasted from 8.0 p.m. till 11.5 p.m. The enemy's retaliation was moderate & directed on our Support Lines & WESTMINSTER BRIDGE ROAD.	
			Casualties:- 18463 Cpl. Halford Wdd 18508 Pte. R Williams } wounded 31408 " T Smith	
	19		Very quiet - nothing unusual happened. Enemy fairly active with rifle grenades.	
			Casualties: 18463 Pte M Hughes } killed 18158 Pte G. Jones 19191 " H.G. Hughes } wounded 31143 " S.E. Latham } 19101 " E.J. Jones	
	20.		About 9.0 p.m. our T.M.F. was attacked by Bombers & 8 men were wounded. They were driven back & never got into the Sap.	
			A listening post near PRINCE'S ISLAND held up a patrol of the enemy (3 strong) who refused to stand up and their leader, a sergeant-major, was shot. This, & papers refused sent to Brigade Headquarters showed that he belonged to the 5th Regt.	

16th Battn Royal Welsh Fus.

February 1916

WAR DIARY
or
INTELLIGENCE SUMMARY

Army Form C. 2118.

Place	Date	Hour	Summary of Events and Information	Remarks and references to Appendices
1st & 2nd CUINCHY	20		Sentries in NEW ROSE St. & SCOTTISH TRENCH gave warning that a large party of Germans were advancing towards our trench; we manned the parapet & they were dispersed by M.G. & rifle fire. About 4.30 pm there was a Trench Gas alarm. There was no delay in having back the warning & no one had put his Gas helmet. Casualties:- 9612496B 2ndLieut 19683 & Pte 1530y L/Cpl. Pte 19807, 18701 E. Evans 31905 Pte nun 12283 & Pte 1946 A Sharp & 18509 C.Shay Kirkham all wounded & 17058 Pte John Jones became attached to us for instruction. Casualties: 1946 A Sharp & 18509. The 14th Battn Lancs. Fusiliers (Bantams) became attached to us for instruction.	
	21		Quiet during morning, just before relief enemy shelled our front line trench. Relief completed at 12:10 am. The whole Battn was relieved by 15th Battn Royal Welch Fus. four small forts were occupied by Battn and into Divisional Reserve at GORRE, with 4 men in each one. no other men in each one. Casualties:- Pte 19878 St Sergeant 2 w/16 Pte John Jones Lieut. E.J. Snell } wounded. Yorpl R Spencer 20519 & Pte 19836 Sgt M Thomas 18655 Pte A Walker 12869 " P Davies killed R.S.Evans 23185 James 24414	
GORRE	22		Cleaning up.	
1st Ref	23		Routine work & baths.	
F3 & Central	24		do	
Redoubt Coulembert	25		Bomber, snipers & signallers left GORRE to relieve the corresponding branches of the 15th R.W.F. at 2.30 km. The remainder of the Battn left GORRE at 6.0 pm & the relief of the 15th Battn R.W.F. in the front line trenches was completed by 9.0 pm. Casualties:- Nil	

Army Form C. 2118.

16th Battn Royal Welsh Fus

WAR DIARY
or
INTELLIGENCE SUMMARY.
(Erase heading not required.)

Instructions regarding War Diaries and Intelligence Summaries are contained in F.S. Regs., Part II. and the Staff Manual respectively. Title pages will be prepared in manuscript.

Place	Date	Hour	Summary of Events and Information	Remarks and references to Appendices
GIVENCHY	26.		Very quiet in the morning. From 1.30 p.m. till 4.40 p.m. the Artillery carried out an offensive operation against the salient about pt A.9.6.24. Enemy artillery retaliated fully, shelling our communication trenches & support trenches. A few Minenwerfer were also sent over in reply to our Trench Mortars. A bombing attack was arranged to be made on the pt bombarded by the Artillery. Two parties went out, one bombing party and one covering party. The Bombers were held up by 3 listening posts of the enemy and as the attack failed. It was supported by Artillery but about 60% of our shells were "duds", consequently very little damage was done. Both parties returned in without loss. The 14th Lancs Fusiliers left us. Casualties: 19819 Pte Williamson } wounded 19328 " Williams } 19418 " Griffiths } 19446 " Jones }	
	27.		Very quiet during the day. A minenwerfer dropped into our trench causing several casualties. The 15th Cheshires (Bantams) joined us for instruction. Casualties: 31016 Pte B Dymott } killed 19118 " a Jones } 26638 " " Hartmon } 18007 Pte Griffiths } 18033 " Evans } wounded 18017 " Beasley } 19820 L/Cpl Casselian } 19049 Pte G.P. Griffiths } killed	
	28.		Very quiet. Casualties: 18273 Pte Snuppiter } wounded 19556 " Hayne }	
	29		Considerable aeroplane & Artillery activity. Relieved by 15th Battn Royal Welsh Fus & went into support in The Village Lines relieving the 14th Battn Royal Welsh Fus.	

2353 Wt. W2544/1454 700,000 5/15 D.D.&L. A.D.S.S./Forms/C. 2118.

1/6th Battn. Royal Welsh Fus.

WAR DIARY
or
INTELLIGENCE SUMMARY.

Army Form C. 2118.

Place	Date	Hour	Summary of Events and Information	Remarks and references to Appendices
GIVENCHY	29		Our dispositions were:—	
			"D" Coy (Capt. HUNKIN). GIVENCHY KEEP 2 off + 50 O.R.	
			HILDER " ½ platoon	
			HERTS " 1 platoon	
			MOAT FARM " ½ platoon	
			Remainder of Coy in billets near WINDY CORNER	
			"C" Coy (Capt. FLETCHER). Billets in Village Lines	
			"B" Coy (Major McLELLAN).. LE PLANTAIN N. 1 off + 1 platoon	
			" S 1 off + 1 platoon	
			Remainder of Coy in Billets in LE PLANTAIN	
			"A" Coy (Capt. PAINE). Billets in WINDY CORNER.	
			H.Q. at point A.14.a.l.3.9. (Ref. Brigade trench map Area F.)	

Ernest Smith Lt Col
O/C 1/6 RWF
1/3/16

16 R. Werk Ins
Vol 4

March 1916

1/4 Batn. Royal Welsh Fus.

Army Form C. 2118.

WAR DIARY
or
INTELLIGENCE SUMMARY.
(Erase heading not required.)

March 1916

Place	Date	Hour	Summary of Events and Information	Remarks and references to Appendices
Bn. H.Q. at Lt. A.14.A.9.b. (Brigade Trench Map Area F)	1		St Davids day. In support in Village Lines. Reliefs &c. Working parties supplied to R.E.s and improvements made to Reliefs &c. Casualties: Nil	
	2		In support - Usual working parties. Casualties: Nil	
	3		In support - Usual working parties. Casualties: Nil	
H.Q. at Lt. A.8.C.2.3 (Brigade Trench Map Area F)	4		Relieved the 15th Batn. Royal Welsh Fus. in the left front line trenches. Our dispositions were:- "B" Co (Major McLellan). 1 company in front line trench from HAMILTON TERR to NEW ROSE ST. "A" Co (Capt. PAINE) 1 platoon in front line trench NEW ROSE ST. 1 platoon in POPPY REDOUBT 2 platoons in NEW CUT and CALEDONIA RD "C" Co (Capt. FLETCHER) 1 platoon in PRINCES ISLAND 1 platoon in GEORGE ST. Remainder in Reserve at LE PLANTIN "D" Co. (Capt: HUNKIN). 1 company in GROUSE BUTTS & COLDSTREAM EXTENSION. Casualties: Nil	
	5		Weather bad - much snow which thawed making trenches very muddy. Work done in pushing saps forward, & building funk-holes in NEW ROSE ST and GROUSE BUTTS. Casualties: Nil	

1st Bttn Royal Welsh Fus

Army Form C. 2118.

WAR DIARY
or
INTELLIGENCE SUMMARY.

March 1916

Place	Date	Hour	Summary of Events and Information	Remarks and references to Appendices
Bn HQ at A.2.C.23. (Brigade Trench Sub Area F)	6		Very quiet. Bombs put down on PRINCES ISLAND. Knock Knee on CHESHIRE ROAD. Casualties - 18983 Pte W Fox. 13 Coy Wounded.	
	7		Very quiet. A new Emma built in PRINCES ISLAND + new emplacts in SCOTTISH TRENCH and POPPY REDOUBT (1st from down UPPER CUT). Casualties: Nil	
	8		Very quiet. One company of the 11th Battn Cheshire Regt attached to us for instruction. Relieved by the 1/5th Battn Welsh Regt and company of 11th Cheshire. 19269 L/Cpt Hoyle 13 Coy wounded. Casualties: 19115, 19552 Goldsworthy, Pierce killed at LA PANNERIE. Regt handed over to them. The whole battalion moved to the Divisional Reserve.	
Bn HQ at W.4.6.4.6. (Bethune Lashed sheet 36.6.)	9		In Divisional Reserve - cleaning up. Routine + fat. put + pads + supplied for working.	
	10		do	do
	11		do	do
	12		do	Routine - Baths + LOCON
	13		do	do
	14		do	do
	15		do	Sunday - no routine
Bn HQ at X.16.d.6.2. (Rutland Camp Sheet 36.6.23)	16		The whole Battn moved to the Brigade Reserve Lines at LE TOURET	Routine
	17		do	Brigade Reserve - Routine + RE working party supplied.
	18		do	do
	19			Relieved the 15th Battn Scinde Rifles Bn in the Right sub-sector.	
	20				

1/6th Batt. Royal Welsh Fus.

WAR DIARY
or
INTELLIGENCE SUMMARY.

Army Form C. 2118.

March 1916

Place	Date	Hour	Summary of Events and Information	Remarks and references to Appendices
Bn. H.Q. A.2.B.2.6. Bridge Trench trap Area G	20		Dispositions were:— "A" Co. (Capt. PAINE). 1 Platoon in GEORGE ST. Remainder in GROUSE BUTTS & COLDSTREAM EXTENSION. "D" Co. (Capt. HUNKIN). 1 Platoon in PRINCE'S ISLAND 1 Platoon in ISLANDS 1-8 inclusive Remainder in OLD BRITISH LINE "B" Co. (Major McLELLAN). 1 Company in OLD BRITISH LINE from pt A.2.B.12.9½ to A.2.D.3.Y. "C" Co. (Capt. ELLIS). 1 Platoon in ISLANDS 9-13 inclusive, Remainder in OLD BRITISH LINE from pt S.26.B.9 to pt A.2.B.12.9½. Casualties:- nil	
	21		Very quiet. Our snipers had a good day, as enemy exposed themselves freely. Much work done on Islands & O.B.L. Working parties supplied to R.E.'s Casualties:- nil	
	22		Very quiet:- Artillery on both sides inactive. Work carried on in O.B.L. and ISLANDS Casualties:- nil	
	23		ditto	
	24		Casualties:- 25334 Pte A/Sgt. Day (accidentally wounded) Weather bad, much snow. Relieved by 15th Bn. Royal Welsh Fus, and went into Support at FESTUBERT.	

Army Form C. 2118.

1st Batt. Royal Welch Fus.

WAR DIARY
or
INTELLIGENCE SUMMARY.
(Erase heading not required.)

March 1916

Instructions regarding War Diaries and Intelligence Summaries are contained in F. S. Regs., Part II and the Staff Manual respectively. Title pages will be prepared in manuscript.

Place	Date	Hour	Summary of Events and Information	Remarks and references to Appendices
Br.H.Q. (S.13.c.5.1.)	25		In support - working parties supplied for R.E's at night. Casualties: - nil	
	26		Casualties: - nil do	
	27		Casualties: - nil do	
Br.H.Q. A.2.A.3.8.	28		Relieved the 15th R.S. Royal Welch Fus. in the right front line. Our dispositions were:- "D" Co (Capt. HUNKIN) . GROUSE BUTTS, GEORGE ST & COLDSTREAM EXTENSION. "A" Co (Capt. PAINE) . Islands 1-8 Inclusive & O.B.L "C" Co (Capt. ELLIS) . O.B.L. "B" Co (Major MCLELLAN). Islands 9-13 Inclusive & O.B.L. Casualties: - nil	
	29		Quiet. Our artillery very quiet. Casualties:- nil	
	30		Quiet - much aeroplane activity. Artillery on both sides quiet. Casualties:- nil	
	31		Hostile artillery very active, ours very quiet.	

16th Battn Royal Welch Fus.

April 1916

Army Form C. 2118.

WAR DIARY
or
INTELLIGENCE SUMMARY.
(Erase heading not required.)

Place	Date	Hour	Summary of Events and Information	Remarks and references to Appendices
April LA PANNERIE	1		2nd Batt. Relieved by 15th Batt. Welsh Regt. The whole Battalion marched back to Divisional Reserve Area at LA PANNERIE.	
	2		Divisional Reserve. Cleaning up.	
	3		do — Routine	
	4		do — do	
	5		do — do	
	6		do — do	
	7		do — do	
	8		do — do	
	9		The whole battalion moved to Brigade Reserve Area at GORRÉ	
GORRÉ	10		Brigade Reserve. On the 11th Machine Gunners were in the line. Support the following Casualties 19599 Pte A Galler - Killer 18031 Pte S.Jones & Robert Wounded 18643 Pte J.Evans	
	11		do	
	12			
	13		Relieved 15th Batt. Royal Welsh Fus. in front line trenches in the GIVENCHY Section. One french mortar batteries carried out a small offensive operation. Every retaliation fairly severe but did no damage. Casualties:- 18977 Cpl Prothroe. Wounded 19357 Pte M Cdewitt 19507 Pte JaEvans	
	14		2nd Lt.	
	15		Relieved by 14th Battn Hants Regt. whole Battn marched back to Divisional Reserve Billets at LA PANNERIE	
	16		The whole battalion marched to ESTAIRES	
	17		Relieved 8th Batn Glosters Regt in front line trenches in the MORTE D GRANGE Sector	

16th Batt Royal Welsh Fus.

WAR DIARY or **INTELLIGENCE SUMMARY**

April XXXVIII

Place	Date	Hour	Summary of Events and Information	Remarks and references to Appendices
Jug at Mr M34.6.594	17		We held the front line from Dead Pig Lane pt M.35.D.51.6 to point M.30.C.2.6 and garrisoned PUMP HOUSE: LA FOSSE POST & TILLELOY SOUTH POST.	
			Casualties: Nil	
	18		Quiet. Casualties: 19266 Sgt. E. Rickert. Wounded	
	19		Quiet. Slight hostile shelling on our left front line trenches. No damage done. Casualties: 2714) Pte H.E. Morton – Killed	
RIEZ BAILLEUL	20		Relieved by 15th Batt. R.W. Fus. & went into Brigade Reserve at RIEZ BAILLEUL. We garrisoned two posts at ROUGE CROIX.	
	21		In Brigade Reserve – Routine: working parties supplied to R.E. at night	
	22		do do	
	23		do do	
	24		Relieved by 15th Batt. Welsh Regt. whole Battalion moved to MERVILLE	
MERVILLE	25		Divisional Reserve – Routine	
	26		do	
	27		do	
	28		do	
	29		do	
	30		do	
LAVENTIE			Bussed to LAVENTIE	

WAR DIARY
or
INTELLIGENCE SUMMARY.

Army Form C. 2118.

Place	Date	Hour	Summary of Events and Information	Remarks and references to Appendices
	31st		Bn. moved from Buysscheure to Setques	

C.G. Jones Lt. Col.
Commanding 16th Rl. Fusiliers

WAR DIARY or **INTELLIGENCE SUMMARY**
Army Form C. 2118.

XXVIII 16 Welsh Fus

Place	Date	Hour	Summary of Events and Information	Remarks and references to Appendices
	May 1st		Relieved 11th Batn. S.W.B. in the front line in the LAVENTIE SECTION.	
			DISTRIBUTION: RIGHT COY. A.COY.	
			Front Line — O.R.	
			" — 120	
			Fireworks Post — 16	
			RIGHT CENTRE COY. B.COY.	
			Front Line — 5 — 144	
			LEFT CENTRE COY. C.COY.	
			Front Line — 3 — 104	
			Flank Post — 45	
			LEFT COY: D COY.	
			Front Line — 5 — 103	
			A.I. Post — 43	
			Battn H. Qrs. — 4 — 35	
			& M.O.	
			Casualties: — Nil	

Army Form C. 2118.

WAR DIARY
or
INTELLIGENCE SUMMARY
(Erase heading not required.)

Place	Date	Hour	Summary of Events and Information	Remarks and references to Appendices
	2/5/16		Quiet in the front line. Considerable shelling in rear, directed chiefly on O.P's and buildings on the RUE TILLELOY	
			CASUALTIES :- 21493 PTE T. DAVIES A Coy. WOUNDED 19083 " J. GRIFFITHS D " "	
	3"		Quiet in front line. Shelling again directed on RUE TILLELOY and neighbourhood. Few large standing patrols out at night for 2 hours - saw no-one. C. Coy's wiring party saw 6 Huns close up to own wire.	
			CASUALTIES :- Nil	
	4"		Fairly quiet. Enemy sent over incendiary shells which set fire to a building & stacks near PLANK POST.	
			CASUALTIES :- 27537 PTE S. POWELL C. Coy WOUNDED 19547 SGT E.T JONES D " " N20 LIEUT JENKINSON C " "	
	5/4		Heavy shelling of our communication trenches some damage done. Attention was also paid to our front line for a short distance to right and left of the junction of PICANTIN AVE and Front line trench. Our artillery retaliation was weak.	
			Relieved by 15th Battn R.W.F. and moved back to Brigade Reserve in LAVENTIE. The following roads were held by us :-	

Army Form C. 2118.

WAR DIARY
or
INTELLIGENCE SUMMARY
(Erase heading not required.)

Place	Date	Hour	Summary of Events and Information	Remarks and references to Appendices
	5/5/16	cont'd	Hougoumont Post - 1 platoon - A Coy Dead End " - 1 " - A " Laventie East " - 2 " - B " Picantin " - 1 " - D " CASUALTIES :- Nil	
	6/5/16		In Brigade Reserve. Working parties supplied to R.E's.	
	7/5/16		In Brigade Reserve. Working parties supplied to R.E's and Baths.	
	8/5/16		DITTO	
	9/5/16		In Brigade Reserve. Working parties supplied during the morning & Baths. Relieved 1st Batln. R.W.F. in the front line trenches. Our dispositions were the same as during previous tour. CASUALTIES:- C.Q.M.S. NEILSON B Coy Wounded 24413 L/Cpl W Dean A Coy W'd 18597 Pte J.A. Clarke A Coy " (acc'd) 19559 " I. Jones C " " 19179 L/Cpl J. Johnson A " "	583P
	10/5/16		Considerable shelling of our front line to which our Artillery retaliated. Shelling was directed chiefly on Rotten Row Comm. Trench, Red Lamp. A Coy's front line, D Coy's front line & Bond Street Comm. Trench. Some damage - a few casualties. CASUALTIES :- Nil	

WAR DIARY
or
INTELLIGENCE SUMMARY

Army Form C. 2118.

(Erase heading not required.)

Place	Date	Hour	Summary of Events and Information	Remarks and references to Appendices
	11/5/16		Quiet. Casualties:- Nil	
	12/5/16		Communication trenches again shelled: also R.1. Post. Casualties:- 37787. Pte R.W. Piper. A Coy. Killed.	
	13/5/16		Quiet. Relieved by 15th Batn R107 regt went into Brigade Reserve in Laventie	
			Dead End Post held by C. Coy 1 platoon	
			Haubourdin " C " 1 "	
			Laventie East " C " 2 "	
			Picantin " B " 1 "	
			Casualties :- Nil	
	14/5/16		Working parties supplied to R.Es	
	15th		"	
	16th		"	
	17th		Relieved by 10th Welch Regt and whole Batn moved to Riencourt Reserve at Merville. Casualty 2/Lt Hymes 17/5/16. Acy. Wounded	
	18th		In Divisional Reserve :- cleaning up	

Army Form C. 2118.

WAR DIARY
or
INTELLIGENCE SUMMARY
(Erase heading not required.)

Instructions regarding War Diaries and Intelligence Summaries are contained in F. S. Regs., Part II. and the Staff Manual respectively. Title Pages will be prepared in manuscript.

Place	Date	Hour	Summary of Events and Information	Remarks and references to Appendices
	19/5/16		Divisional Reserve. Routine and Working Parties	
	20/5/16		DITTO	
	21/5/16		DITTO	
	22/5/16		DITTO	
	23/5/16		DITTO	Casualty 31406 Pte O'William. Killed
	24/5/16		DITTO	
	25/5/16		Whole Batta. moved to Brigade Reserve Area at RIEZ BAILLEUL.	
	26"		1 Coy in forts in forward area. Remainder of Batta. training and R.E. fatigue parties	
	27"		DITTO	
	28"		DITTO	

5856

Army Form C. 2118.

WAR DIARY
or
INTELLIGENCE SUMMARY
(Erase heading not required.)

Place	Date	Hour	Summary of Events and Information	Remarks and references to Appendices
	29/9/16		Relieved 15th Battn R.W.F. in right sub-section of MARTINSART GRANGE.	
			DISPOSITION:- 3 Coys (A.B.C.) in front line	
			1 Coy - D. in support trencher	
			TRENCH RIFLES 545	
			N° of Officers & men in front	
			line Support & Battn H.Q.s 722.	
			STRENGTH behind with TRANSPORT 87	
			CASUALTIES:- Nil	
	30th		Quiet day. Slight enemy shelling. At 7.30p.m enemy commenced intense bombardment on Brigade on immediate right and heavily shelled our battn area and that of the 13th R.W.F. on our left. The bombardment lasted from 7.30 to about 9.35 p.m. The enemy shelled over a very large area and our front line trenches were only slightly damaged. Casualties which were slight were as follows:-	
			Killed: 19618 Pte W.Edwards	
			Wounded: L/Cpl W.Paine	
			19325 Pte W.R.Brown	
			19601 Sgt G.Earle	
			A: 24855 L/Cpl W.Hendon	
			" 18731 Pte H.G.Benton	

WAR DIARY
or
INTELLIGENCE SUMMARY

Army Form C. 2118.

Place	Date	Hour	Summary of Events and Information	Remarks and references to Appendices
	31/5/16		A very quiet day. Enemy hardly fired a shot even. About mid-night on right Coy sent a bombing party to crater, opposite "Dicks Bill", occupied by the Germans. M 36 A 4.1. The party, 18 strong under 2/Lt Hughes threw 50 bombs into a German working party and caused considerable casualties. Our own casualties, from bombs & machine gun fire were:- 2 killed - 5 wounded; as below:- Killed: 10073 Pte S.J. Phillips, 19651 " W.L. Thomas. Wounded: 18281 Sgt J. Hughes, 26574 Pte H. Fildes, 34895 " J.R. Bell, 19304 " W. Davies, 19253 " D. James.	

R.A.B. Fairfull Col
O/C 16 Welsh Regt
1/6/16

June 1916   16th R.W.F.   WAR DIARY or INTELLIGENCE SUMMARY   XXXVIII 1/3/38   Army Form C.2118.

16. R. Welsh Fus

Vol 7

Place	Date	Hour	Summary of Events and Information	Remarks and references to Appendices
MATED GRANGE.	1		Considerable hostile artillery - no damage done.	
	2		do Relieved by 15th R.W.F. in front line trenches + went into Brigade Reserve area at RIEZ BAILLEUL	
	3		In Brigade Reserve	
	4		do	
	5		do	
	6		do	
	7		do	
	8		Relieved the 15th R.W.F. in front line trench.	
	9		"	
	10		Relieved by 2/8th Worcesters.	
	11		Arrived in LA GORGUE	
	12		" " BELLE RIVE	
	13		" " RAIMBERT.	
	14		Arrived in OSTREUILLE	
	15			

June 1916. 16 K.R.W.?.

Army Form C. 2118.

WAR DIARY
or
INTELLIGENCE SUMMARY
(Erase heading not required.)

Instructions regarding War Diaries and Intelligence Summaries are contained in F. S. Regs., Part II. and the Staff Manual respectively. Title Pages will be prepared in manuscript.

Place	Date	Hour	Summary of Events and Information	Remarks and references to Appendices
OSTREUILLE	16		Training	
	17		"	
	18		"	
	19		"	
	20		"	
	21		"	
	22		"	
	23		"	
	24		"	
	25		"	
	26		Left OSTREVILLE for BUIRE-AU-BOIS. Arrived at BUIRE-AU-BOIS.	
	27		" PROUVILLE	
	28		cleaning up	
	29			
	30		Left BROUVILLE for PUCHEVILLERS.	

Casualties. June 2nd 1916 { 19469 Sgt/Jones Volunteer accts
16488 Cpl F.Evans
23365 Pte N.Hayles
18557 - D'Roberts
3669 - Harry Wilmer
18153 - NW Price
9th 1916 19146 - R.O. Jones Killed
" - 23024 - WH Edwards Wounded
" - 37281 - A Edwards -
" 10 - - -

June 11th 1916. Wounded
18824 Pte Chillins
24398 Afzal Janizan
1837 - reported
June 11th 1916. Wounded
Currenther Emm
Ostwand Sr.

113th Inf.Bde.
38th Div.

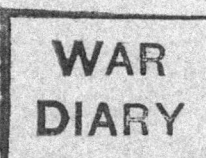

16th BATTN. THE ROYAL WELCH FUSILIERS.

J U L Y

1 9 1 6

Box 2556

Attached:

Appendix I.
(Report on Operations
in Mametz Wood).

Army Form C. 2118.

Vol 8

113/38

WAR DIARY
or
INTELLIGENCE SUMMARY.
(Erase heading not required.)

Place	Date	Hour	Summary of Events and Information	Remarks and references to Appendices

WAR DIARY for JULY 1916

16 BATT. R.W.F.

1/4th Royal Welsh Fus. July 1916 Army Form C. 2118.

WAR DIARY or INTELLIGENCE SUMMARY

Place	Date	Hour	Summary of Events and Information	Remarks and references to Appendices
	1		Left PUCHEVILLERS. Arrived at LA ELUVILLERS.	
	2		Arrived at RIBEMONT.	
	3		At RIBEMONT.	
	4		Batt. composed of 15 off. + 600 OR. left RIBEMONT and relieved the 2nd S. Staff. in trenches between MAMETZ and MAMETZ WOOD. Remainder of Batt. went to MORLANCOURT. Relief complete by 10.0 p.m.	
	5		Casualties ½ line moving & reconnoitring of trenches & made a dispositions. Withdrawn from line near CARNOY. Killed 3 O.R. Wounded 24 Other Ranks 18 Other Ranks	
	6		Relieved the 10th Batt. R.W. 3 p.m front line trenches. Casualties nil.	
	7		Quiet. Casualties nil.	
	8		Some shelling. Preparing for attack to take place on the 10th. Casualties nil.	
	9		At 3.0 am the Battn formed up in 8 lines 500 yds from the Southern edge of MAMETZ WOOD. The 114 & 15th B were on the right flank. The attack was launched at 4.20 am & a footing was gained in the wood by 5.0 am a considerable portion of the wood was in our hands. The Battn was dug in itself on when relieved by the 13th R.W.F. to relief the Battn withdrew to the original front line trenches. Killed Major Jones (wounded) Reported Missing Lt Z. Peacock 6th other ranks. Capt. S. Z. W. F. Rees Lt Other Ranks " Depaunt " S. Falconbridge Lt Humphries 92 " " D. Robinson 186 Other Ranks Casualties..	See Appendix II

WAR DIARY or INTELLIGENCE SUMMARY

Army Form C. 2118.

1/4th Royal Welch Fusiliers
July 1916

Place	Date	Hour	Summary of Events and Information	Remarks and references to Appendices
	11		Relieved the 13th & 15th Battns R.W.F. in the wood. During the day the remainder of the wood fell into our hands & we consolidated the northern & north-eastern edge. At 10 p.m. relief was due by the 10th Northumberland Fusiliers who did not stop to relieve but whole strength & attacked the enemy's second defence system, consequently delayed in relief.	
	12		Cavalliere. The Batn was withdrawn from the wood by 12 noon & marched to join the remainder after Bn left behind at MORANCOURT. The whole Battn bivouaced at GRIVETOIN. W.I. Cavallie.	
	13		The Battn detrained at LONGPRE & marched to AILLY-le-H-CLOCHER	
	14		Arrived at BRUCAMPS	
	15		Arrived by train at ST. LEGER - Lee - AUTH 'IE	
	16		At ST LEGER	
	17		1 detachment of 11 officers + 200 o/r's marched to + bivouaced at COVIN. The Battn with detachments from the 13th & 14th marched to + bivouaced at MAILLY - MAILLET.	
	18		Working parties supplied to 252 Tunnelling Coy R.E. detachment from COVIN marched to COIGNEUX	
	19		detachment at COIGNEUX marched to MAILLY-MAILLET to rejoin the Batt'n working parties supplied.	

16th Batt. Royal Welsh Fus.

Army Form C. 2118.

WAR DIARY
INTELLIGENCE SUMMARY

July 1916

Place	Date	Hour	Summary of Events and Information	Remarks and references to Appendices
MAILLY/MAILLET	20 28		MAILLY WOOD. Working parties supplied to 252 Tunnelling Co. R.E. On the 23rd the detachment from 15th R.W.F. rejoined its Battalion. CASUALTIES:- 2 O.R. WOUNDED. 1 Officer 2nd Lt. I.D. REES, WOUNDED. Battalion moved to BUSSLES ARTOIS.	
	28			
	29		— moved to billets at THIEVRES.	
	30		Evening marched to DOULLENS & entrained there.	
	31		Detrained at HOPOUTRE & from there marched to HERZEELE where we entered billets.	

A. G. Prue Major
16th R.W.F.
Comdg.

A P P E N D I X   I.

(Report on Operations in
Mametz Wood).

APPENDIX I

OPERATIONS IN MAMETZ WOOD.

10R. & 11R. July 1916.

At 3 a.m. on the morning of the 10th the Battalion left QUEEN'S NULLAH to take up a position of readiness on the hill-top facing MAMETZ WOOD. Our orders were to advance from there against the western face of the wood to force an entry and then to swing round to the R. and establish a line facing N. on a pre-arranged position. A special party of bombers had been arranged to deal with STRIP TRENCH.

The advance was to begin at H/12 a.m. in eight lines of men extended to H. hours at distances of 50 to 100 yds. between lines, and the whole movement to be carried out in conjunction with the 114th Brigade on our R.

Shortly before 4 a.m. Col. Carden went to the 114th Brigade, intending to return to the Battalion when it was

taking form had let us know. At 4.30 a.m. the Battn. left from its position with Coys and the Brigade on our right seemed to have completely moved off. I tried to find the Colonel but could only learn that he had not returned. Concluding that he had become a casualty, I gave the word to advance.

On reaching the brow of the hill, the leading lines saw the 114th Brigade, or parts of it, retiring, and they too wavered. Somewhat forward, but shewn all churned to their previous positions. This was not a halting flight, but was done slowly and also largely owing to some one who cannot (be traced) raising a shout of "Retire".

Almost immediately after this Col. Carden returned and the advance began again.

Captain G.C. Westhouse and Lt A.V. Read Gr had shown great coolness in pulling their men together, and this time the movement now carried out in good order. As the officers stated that the advance down the hill into under heavy artillery and machine gun fire was executed with few first casualties.

At the foot of the hill there was a little clear ground, and then came the advance across the open against the edge of the wood. The enemy were not well prepared for an attack from this direction, but he had a shallow firing trench from which he inflicted severe casualties by his rifle fire. Col Corden was wounded at this stage of the attack, but went on until he received a final and mortal wound.

Once our line had reached

little
the enemy positions resistance was encountered, and the enemy surrendered in large numbers.

Meanwhile the bombers were successfully attacking STRAP TRENCH, and though their losses were severe, including 2/Lt H.H.T. Ross, they can (and) to push on and hit the British was cleared. They required some aid from the infantry, many of whom had pushed straight through the wood.

For some time after this the attack was wanting in organization, small parties pushing out in all directions in search of the enemy. Eventually about 6:30 a.m. a hill was formed across the wood, and the men were organised. The 16th. then held the extreme left section of the line.

Patrols were pushed out

from this line and cleared away
in all groups of the enemy who
were still firing, but a further
advance was impossible, as our
own artillery was firing onwards
and many of the shells burst about
80 yards in front of our line.
The line was rather cramped,
and about 1 p.m. the 16th R.W.?
was ordered to withdraw to QUEEN'S
NULLAH.

11th July. On the morning of the 11th
the Batt. returned to MAMETZ
WOOD at 9 a.m. and took up
a position along the railway
between the points marked O-K
on the specially issued map,
i.e. from the Strong point
on the W. face of the wood to
a point 250 yards N.E.
We entrenched along this line.
At 4 p.m. orders were issued for
an advance to the edge of the

Wood, and patrols were sent out.
A battalion on our right moved at
6 p.m. and we advanced at the
same time; the ground had been
abandoned by the enemy.
Close to the edge of the wood we
entrenched, and in that position we
remained until relieved at 8.30
a.m. on the 12th.
There was fairly heavy shelling
during the night 11th to 12th and
the early morning of the 12th,
but we suffered no casualties.

J.R. Gatehouse Major
16th R.W.F.

Vol 9

16 Batt. RWF

War Diary for August 1916

WAR DIARY
or
INTELLIGENCE SUMMARY

(Erase heading not required.)

Army Form C. 2118.

16th Royal Welsh Fusiliers.

113th Inf. Bde. 38th (Welsh) Div. VIII Corps.

Place	Date	Hour	Summary of Events and Information	Remarks and references to Appendices
	August 1917			
	3		Reported arrival:- 2/Lt R.L. MANN, D.A. MORRIS, G. NEAL	(A.1)
	17		Battalion marched from HERZEELE to K camp (S.W. of POPERINGHE) Sheet 27 L 2 a 5.4	
	3rd 6 19th		Reported arrival 2/Lt G.J. RING. Training in K camp, efforts concentrated on training new specialists.	(A.2)
	20		To Trenches. Entrained at POPERINGHE midnight 20/21, detrained at ASYLUM SDG YPRES. Marched to Trenches a.r	(A.2)
	21		Sheet 28 squares 7a, 13a. Took over from 2nd Seaforth Highlanders, relief complete 4 a.m. Battalion in left sub-sector of brigade. 14th R.W.F. on right, French Army on left. Turn gas alarm 8 pm. 11 pm respectively.	A.2.
	22		Casualties - Killed 1 O.R. - Wounded 1 O.R.	
	23		Stock H. strength sent to England. 2/Lt A.A. HAGUE. Casualties - Killed 1 O.R.	
	24		Relieved in front line by 15th R.W.F. Relief complete 11 p.m. Battalion to support dugouts on W. bank of CANAL	
	28		Battalion to front line in relief of 15th R.W.F. in same sub-sector. Reported arrival:- Lt D.E. DAVIES. 2/Lts A.J. MURPHY, A.N. GRIFFITHS, A.H. DAWKES.	
			Casualties:- 1 O.R. wounded. Strike off strength:- Maj. H.M. Richards.	
	29		Gas alarm 11.30 p.m.	
	30		Casualties:- Killed 1 O.R. Draft of 47 O.R. reported arrival.	
	31		Casualties:- Killed Lt T.D. TANNER - Wounded 1 O.R.	

A.A. Jones Lt. Col.
Comdg. 16 R.W.F.

WAR DIARY
16th BATTALION R.W.F.
FOR SEPTEMBER 1916

Army Form C. 2118.

16th Bn Royal Welsh Fusiliers
113th Inf Bde 38th (Welsh) Division
VIII (8) B165

WAR DIARY
or
INTELLIGENCE SUMMARY
(Erase heading not required.)

Place	Date	Hour	Summary of Events and Information	Remarks and references to Appendices
	September 1st		Relieved by 15th Bn R.I.Fusiliers in front line, left subsection evacuated – Nil	
	2nd /16 5th		Support Battn. To send up same working parties as before to A.E.S. and front line Battn. Casualties – Nil	
	5/9/16		Relieved by 10th Battn S. Borderers 113th Bde. Marched to "J" Camp. Divisional Reserve arriving about 5 am 6/9/16	
	6th /16 15th		Divisional Reserve "J" Camp. Working Parties (several days) assisted to A.S. for front line and training & sundry fatigues other days. Casualties. 1 O.R. wounded on Working Party	
			Reinforcements 11th { Capt. I. Griffith and 2/Lt I.G. Bevan 12th { 2/Lt Williams + 2/Lt Ed. Koos 15th { 2/Lt C. Jones	
			Other { 9th 30. O.R. from 10th Welsh Regt. Ranks {10th 18 " " 15th 3 (3) new draft (10) old men rejoined no men rejoined	
	Nov 19 17		Relieved 11th R.W.F. Left support battn. Left subsection	

Army Form C. 2118.

WAR DIARY
or
INTELLIGENCE SUMMARY.
(Erase heading not required.)

Instructions regarding War Diaries and Intelligence Summaries are contained in F.S. Regs., Part II. and the Staff Manual respectively. Title pages will be prepared in manuscript.

Place	Date	Hour	Summary of Events and Information	Remarks and references to Appendices
	11th		Relieved 10th K.O.B. in front line.	
	18th to 22nd		Bn in front line. Situation quiet. Casualties :- Nil.	
	22/23		Battn relieved in front line by 1st Bn R.W.Kts	
	23rd to 27th		Left subsection Battn Working parties supplied to R.E. Casualties - Nil	
	27/28		Relieved 1st Bn R.W.Kts in front line. Front line. Situation quiet.	
	29		" "	
	30		" " Considerable enemy activity on our line, our artillery retaliating. Casualties :- 1 O.R. killed 10 O.R. Wounded.	

Vol II

WAR DIARY.

16TH BATT: ROYAL WELSH FUSILIERS

OCTOBER 1916

Army Form C. 2118.

WAR DIARY
or
INTELLIGENCE SUMMARY
(Erase heading not required.)

16th Bn. Royal Welsh Fusiliers
113th Inf. Bde. 38th Division
VIII Corps

Instructions regarding War Diaries and Intelligence Summaries are contained in F. S. Regs., Part II. and the Staff Manual respectively. Title Pages will be prepared in manuscript.

Place	Date	Hour	Summary of Events and Information	Remarks and references to Appendices
Left subsector	OCTOBER 1st		Battn relieved whole line, left subsector, by 15th Bn. R.W.F. and moved to support dugouts on N. Bank of Canal. Casualties 1st to 5th:— Killed 1 O.R. Wounded 3 O.R.	
"	3rd		Relieved 15th R.W.F. in front line, same subsector:— Casualties 5th to 9th:— Killed — 2nd Lt. R. L. Mann 1 O.R. D. of Wds 1 O.R. Wounded 3 O.R.	
"	9th		Battn relieved in front line by 15th R.W.F. and moved to support dugouts on N. bank of Canal:— Casualties 9th to 14th:— Killed — Wounded 3 O.R.	
"	14th		Relieved 15th Bn. R.W.F. in front line:—	
"	15th		The Battn was relieved in front line by 10th Bn. Welsh and succeeded to take over Right Reserve station — right sub-sector, relief by 13th Welsh Regt. Three officers and sixty O.R. withdrawn from Battn to form Raiding Party. They proceeded to Baux D for Special training. Casualties 15th to 19th — 2nd Lt. Wounded. Capt. G.D. Ellis	
Right Subsector	19th		Relieved by 14th Bn. R.W.F. Battn entrained at Ypres Asylum about 9.45 p.m. detrained at Peselhoek 10.15 p.m. arriving at 'P' Camp about 10.30 p.m.	

WAR DIARY
or
INTELLIGENCE SUMMARY
(Erase heading not required.)

Army Form C. 2118.

Place	Date	Hour	Summary of Events and Information	Remarks and references to Appendices
Camp 'P'	20th	6.25 PM	Training carried out. Working parties supplied for cable-trenching also parties supplied to R.E. Casualties :- Nil. Nine men volunteer for raiding party	
1st Subsector	25th		Took over support position - left subsector from 15th Bn R Ir.R. Casualties 3 O.R. wounded 25" × 16 " 1 " " (died) 29 × 16	
	29/30		Raid on enemies trenches carried out in accordance with scheme submitted Reuters: see Scheme A	
	30		Relieved 15th Bn.R.Ir.R in front line. casualties 29th × 30th O.R. 1 Killed 1 Missing 7 Wounded	

1/10/16

WAlex
Lieut Col
Commanding
1st Bn Royal Irish Fusiliers

REPORT ON RAID MADE BY 16TH ROYAL WELSH FUSILIERS
ON NIGHT OF 29TH - 30TH OCTOBER, 1916.

Everything unusually quiet until 10-30 p.m. From then onwards our machine guns on CANAL BANK and elsewhere kept up an intermittent fire. The Raiders were reported as being in position at Jumping Off point before 11-0 p.m. At 11-19 p.m. the bombardment of the junction of CACTUS and CABLE TRENCHES by our field guns and howitzers commenced, and lifted about 11-23 to a barrage surrounding that point.

Two minutes after the bombardment began, enemy machine guns from trenches West of FARM 14, and from direction of CADDIE TRENCH opened a heavy fire on NO MAN'S LAND, ESSEX and WHITE TRENCHES and the CANAL BANK. A machine gun also swept down the CANAL as far as BRIDGE 6.D.,(where one sentry was killed). I believe there were no casualties from this fire among raiders, probably because they were already very close to the enemy wire.

At 11-27 the German Artillery opened on ESSEX TRENCH with light H.E. and Shrapnel, (probably ·77 mms.). At same time Belgian Trench Mortars began to fire very heavily on CABLE TRENCH.

At 11-33 Germans shelled ESSEX, WHITE and FARGATE TRENCHES with ·77 mms. Their Trench Mortars opened on point of exit in ESSEX TRENCH.

At 11-35 p.m. FARGATE is heavily shelled (believed with 5·9's) and a heavy bombardment of our trenches C.14.10., C.14.11., and C.14.12, with shrapnel and with ·77 mm.H.E. is begun.

11-39. Enemy green light, followed by hooters from direction of CACTUS and CABLE TRENCHES (seen from O.P.)

11-44. Enemy barrage with ·77 mms. and a few 5·9's on BARNSLEY ROAD, CORRIDOR becomes heavier and fire on front slackens

(2)

At same time a barrage of ·77 mm. H.E. and shrapnel was formed West of the CANAL on the open fields between the CANAL and the road South of COLENSO FARM. About 6 shells per minute fell here, and a considerable number of shells fell on, and beyond the road, near the "A" Line and railway. This continued, with a slight pause about midnight, till 12-40 a.m. No shells hit the West bank of the CANAL, and the CANAL was not seriously shelled below BRIDGE 6.2.

At 11-47 p.m. the raiders began to return to our trench. Their telephone wire was broken. (For unknown reason the Battalion making the raid got the message that the raiders had not returned to trench at 12-15 a.m., five minutes before the first prisoner reached the Headquarters. This accounts for the delay in news reaching the Corps)

11-48 p.m. 3 green lights and one red light sent up by enemy behind point raided. After this enemy shelled front line from WHITE to ESSEX TRENCH, harder and with heavier guns.

12-0 a.m. Enemy's fire on these trenches and on FARGATE slackened.

There were very few (if any) casualties in our front line and in FARGATE. I sent two men to inspect these trenches this morning, and they said that the damage was small, as there had been very few direct hits. The enemy's firing must have been very wild: mostly over, I think. The enemy fire on C.14.10. and C.14.12 slackened towards midnight, and at 12-6 a.m. our howitzers and field guns retaliated on enemy trenches South of KRUPP FARM.

12-13 a.m. Green light sent up from CAESAR'S NOSE.

12-14 a.m. Orange and green light sent from direction of CANAL AVENUE. (No result observed)

(3)

Enemy's machine gun fire continuous since 11-30 p.m. on CANAL BANK as far South as BRIDGE 6.

12-40 a.m. Enemy's machine gun and artillery fire ceases.

12-50 a.m. The O.C. LEFT Reserve Battalion requested Artillery to stop their barrage.

12-45 a.m. All quiet.

During the bombardment BRIDGE 6.Z was broken by a 5.9" shell, presumably after midnight, as our raiding party returned by it. No other bridges hit.

DETAILS OF RAID AS COLLECTED FROM RAIDING PARTY.
===

There was practically no enemy resistance. Only 3 men and 1 officer were met. The 3 men surrendered -- the officer (their Company Commander) was shot.

Some men in dugouts were bombed. The remainder got away, as both raiders and prisoners testify. A heavier barrage until 11-30 p.m. would have prevented this.

The German trench was a very poor one -- worse than ours. It was revetted with hurdles and willow gabions, very shallow and not bullet proof.

As far as I could find out, no German bodies were found: total number of Germans killed in dugouts was perhaps 6 to 10. On the left a trench mortar (diameter of muzzle about 9") was found and destroyed. A machine gun is said to have been destroyed and thrown into the wire on the right, but I doubt if this true.

Raiders spent 15 minutes in trench. Casualties:- 3 men wounded: 2 slightly, none very seriously.

Two of the prisoners were unwilling to be led in, and had to be persuaded by tying ropes round their necks.

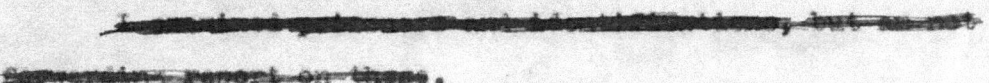

(Signed) G. BRENAN, Lieut.

Officer in charge No 3. O.P.

REPORT OF RAID CARRIED OUT BY

16th BATTN R.W.FUSILIERS

ON NIGHT 29/30th OCT.1916.

1. **PREPARATION.** 3 Officers and 60 O.R. were withdrawn from the Battn on the night 15/16th Oct 1916 and sent to D Camp to prepare for the Raid.

   A scheme was made out, and an exact replica of the German trenches was dug, wire being added.

   The men were given the usual forms of Infantry training, also special instruction in Bayonet fighting, Bombing and Crawling. Much attention was paid to discipline.

   On the night of 25th Oct, as a result of a Conference at 2nd Army Hd.Qrs, the numbers and scope of the Raid were enlarged and a new scheme was made out.

   This scheme has already been submitted, and is referred to in the Narrative.

   On Seven successive nights Officers patrols were sent out to reconnoitre the point to be raided and the intervening ground between it and our trenches.

   Besides this, all men were sent out into No Man's Land in turn, in the form of fighting patrols, ten to fifteen strong, to accustom them to being in the open near the enemy.

2. **NARRATIVE.** A Reconnoitring patrol of One Officer, One N.C.O. and 4 Men, left our trenches at 7.45.p.m. and moved to 'Jumping Off' point. From here 2 men laid a tape back to the 'point of exit' from our trenches.

   The remainder marked 'Jumping Off' point with 2 luminous discs, and then moved out to the German wire at the point to be raided.

   They stayed there some time and reconnoitred to the right and left to make sure that they had selected the right spot. They then laid the tape back to the 'jumping off' point, and in order to make certain that the 'point of entry' had been marked in the right place, they again went back to the German wire, and being satisfied, returned to the 'jumping off' point about 10.30.p.m., meeting the Raiders half-way across No Man's Land at 10.50.p.m.

   They then returned to the 'point of exit' as arranged.

   The Raiding party left the point of Assembly at 9.30. p.m. and moved out to 'point of exit', reaching it at 10.25.p.m. The Officer in charge waited in our trenches for ten minutes to see if the reconnoitring patrol was coming in and then moved out 'point of exit' into No Man's Land in 3 columns, as arranged, the centre-column following the tape.

   Having crossed our wire, the columns were halted for ten minutes to ensure that every man was in his place and out of the trenches, after which the whole moved forward.

   No difficulties were encountered as far as the 'jumping off' point, which was reached at 11.16.p.m.

   At 11.20½ p.m. (½ minute after zero) the party left the 'jumping-off' point and moved along the tape towards the German trenches. Now the ground became very difficult and the men carrying the mats were continually falling into shell holes.

   The columns moved to within 20yds of the wire, beyond which it was found unsafe to go, on account of our bombardment.

NARRATIVE (Contd).

At 11.24.p.m. the bombardment shifted to barrage and the Raiders, quickening the pace, moved up to the German wire.

The left party got into difficulty with their mat on account of the irregularity of the wire: they eventually crossed over by the same mat as the centre party

Beyond the wire the ground was very cut up and odd ends of the wire, and displaced knife rests, lay about: there was a confusion of shell holes, and the ground was soft and boggy, having been ploughed up by the bombardment.

This caused five minutes delay in entering the German trenches.

The parties entered the trenches in the order as arranged, and the Blockers proceeded along to their appointed places to make the blocks. The trenches were so broken in places as to delay progress.

B Blockers reached their appointed place where they had some bombs thrown at them.

E Blockers encountered some resistance and only reached their appointed place as the bugle sounded for the withdrawal.

Three of them were wounded by German bombs, thrown at them from an Easterly direction.

A Blockers got into difficulties in N Trench and did not reach their appointed place.

C Blockers found the trench leading from K and L trenches to their appointed block so broken as to make it impassable to either friend or enemy. They, thereupon, moved along K trench.

Here they found 2 dug-outs: the first yielded 2 prisoners: the second seemed to be an Officers' or N.C.Os' dug-out: One man who was in there offered resistance and was shot.

Another was hiding behind the door and was trying to open his Clasp knife. A tap with a Knob Kerry persuaded him to surrender.

The Clearers mopped up the trenches which were to be cleared and saw 3 enemy dead, including the man killed by the N.C.O. in charge of C Blockers.

The telephonists got into difficulties crossing the wire. They laid a line up to the 'point of entry' but did not succeed in getting communication, the wire having been damaged.

The wounded men of E Blockers were carried across No Man's Land on the backs of other men. The ground was too uneven for the use of Stretchers.

The withdrawal was carried out in order, as arranged, and without confusion, covered by the Reserve under the O.C.Raid.

The right party took rather longer to withdraw than the left.

The Reserve, during the retirement, gathered up the tape.

3. GERMAN TRENCHES AND DUGOUTS.

The German trenches were found to be an average of six feet deep, revetted with a sort of 'wattle'. They were considerably damaged by our fire. They were dry and boarded with duck-boards.

Some dugouts were found, as shown on attached map.

There were two dugouts in H, which were splinter-proof, entrances facing East.

There were two similar dugouts in F, which had been demolished by our fire.

There was a Bomb Store in K, near junction with M, facing North.

There were two dugouts in K in which prisoners were captured, entrances facing South east: both splinter-proof, but not

No. 3 (Contd).

Bomb-proof.

There were 2 dugouts in I, between junction of J and Block E: one was splinter proof: the other was a deep dugout with about 20 steps.

Both these last two had lights in them but were empty.

There were a few shelters along the front line, in the parapet, with overhead weatherproof cover and large enough to admit one man sitting.

There was a slot for a sentry at the point marked Z, with rainproof overhead cover.

The communicating trench North of E appeared to be open ground.

The splinter dugouts were five feet high with about two feet of earth over them, roofs being shored up with pit-props.

No. 4. GERMAN WIRE. The German wire varied from seven to ten yards in depth. It was found to consist of knife rests and some of these had been displaced by bombardment.

It was difficult to see where it began or ended.

It had been well cut about by the bombardment and with the aid of the mats, no difficulty was found in crossing it.

No. 5. ARTILLERY FIRE. The fire of our Artillery was remarkably accurate and well timed.

The enemy seemed to have fired a few shrapnel on No Man's Land after the Raiders entered it.

Three blind enemy shells fell close to our parties when they reached our wire on withdrawal.

Most of the enemy's retaliation seemed to be against the Canal Bank.

No. 6. MACHINE GUNS. Our flanks were well protected by our own Machine Guns sweeping No Man's Land.

There was one short burst of enemy machine gun fire from E (possibly from Fortuin 17) as the raiders were entering the enemy's trenches.

As the tail end of the raiders was re-entering our own trenches, a little enemy machine gun fire came from a North-westerly direction, from the Canal Bank.

No. 7. OBSERVATIONS AND SUGGESTIONS WHICH MIGHT BE USEFUL FOR FUTURE RAIDS.

It would have been better to have timed our withdrawal ten minutes later, allowing thirty minutes in enemy's trench.

It was found that when the raiders first entered the trench, there were too many men bunched about the 'point of entry'.

It would perhaps have been better to have made the Reserve lie down half way between the enemy's wire and the 'point of entry'.

When the reserve entered the trenches it was found that the large numbers tended to block them, especially as there was delay in the Blockers extending to their appointed station

The arrangement for Clearers was found suitable and worked well.

Two sentries were posted, one on either side of the 'point of entry', to check our parties when they withdrew.

These were found to be of no assistance, as they were not able to keep the check properly.

The Ladders were not required, as the trench had been blown in.

No. 7 (Contd).

The Stretcher Bearers, as such, were not of much assistance, as Stretchers could not be used in the dark, among the shell holes in No Man's Land.

It would have been better to have left the Stretchers at the 'point of entry' and had men specially detailed to carry out the wirecutting part of the Stretcher Bearers' task.

The arrangement of the Escort taking over prisoners from the Clearers worked satisfactorily, and the number of the Escort was suitable.

The telephonists were of no assistance as they could not obtain connection owing to the line going wrong.

I had omitted to request the French not to send up Parachute lights, and these gave some trouble to the Raiders when they were going out.

The bugle signal for the withdrawal was found satisfactory.

The torches issued were not satisfactory: more than half were out of working order before starting.
Those which did work were most useful, and in fact, indispensable.
Some system of fixing the torch on the rifle would be very useful, provided it could be made perfectly secure from being accidentally switched on.

N.C.Os should be equipped with revolvers rather than Rifle and Bayonet. These were not obtainable for the raid in time for instruction.

All ranks found the Knob kerry very useful.handy.

The system of carrying 19 bombs in a haversack on the chest, slung by valise straps, one round the neck and one round the waist, was found good.
The bombs make no noise when carried like this.

No use was found for smoke bombs.

Concertina wire was not required, as the trenches were already blown in. The wire used was very useful.

A Very pistol and some lights were issued to the Lewis Gunners at the last moment. These were not used.

The arrangement for Stretcher Bearers widening the gap in the enemy's wire and marking it with luminous discs, was found useful.

The different recognition marks of the three columns was found useful, especially when the left and centre columns had to cross the wire by the same mat.

The lamps hung on a tree on the Canal for guide were not found of much assistance, as they kept on blowing out.
Those who lost the tape found the French parachute lights a guide to their direction.

No. 7. (Contd).

    Clean white tape was found, by experiment beforehand, to be too conspicuous.
    Dirtied tape was used from the enemy's wire to 'jumping off' point, and clean tape back from there.
    When laying the tape, it should be securely pegged, as often it was picked up and used as a guide line in the hand.

8. CASUALTIES.   1 MISSING.
                    5 WOUNDED.

Sgd A.G. Jones
Lieut Col.
Commanding.
16th Battn Royal W. Fusiliers.

30.10.16.

VIII CORPS

SECRET

VIII CORPS
G. 4063.

16 RWFus:
Oct 1916

On the 26th instant the German front line trenches in C.7.c were bombarded with Trench Mortars and Artillery, and parapet and wire were considerably knocked about. The wire was cut opposite the point of entry on the 28th and 29th inst. On the 29th instant the Artillery made certain that the wire at C.7.c,$5\frac{1}{2}.7\frac{1}{2}$ was properly cut.

A patrol of the 16th R.W.F. left our trenches opposite this point at 7-45 p.m. and reached the German wire at 9-0 p.m. The Officer in charge had selected the right point of entry into the German trench, and laid a tape back from this point to the jumping off point in NO MANS LAND.

A raiding party of the 16th R.W.F. (strength 3 officers and 116 O.R.) left our trenches at 10-35 p.m., met the reconnoitring patrol in NO MANS LAND and reached the jumping off point at 11-15 p.m. without encountering any difficulties.

At zero hour (11-20 p.m.) the raiders moved forward in respective parties under cover of Artillery fire. As our Artillery fire lifted the raiders advanced finding the ground very difficult. The enemy's wire which appeared to consist of two lines, was found badly cut, and no difficulty was experienced in getting through it.

Owing however, to the fact that the trenches were so badly knocked about, there was some delay in entering them, and in moving along them especially on the right.

The blocking parties did not in all cases quite reach the points allotted to them, owing to the trenches having been blocked by our Artillery bombardment, but the trenches marked out to be cleared were all cleared.

The German trenches were found to be lightly held and there were several empty dugouts which showed no signs of occupation. Several Germans were found in the trenches killed by our bombardment, and more were killed by our bombers. There were no signs of an enemy machine gun.

3 prisoners of the 3rd Battalion, 86th Reserve Infantry Regiment, 18th Reserve Division were captured.

On the signal being given, the Raiders withdrew to our trenches. All the arrangements worked well.

Our casualties were 4 (four) O.R. slightly wounded.

The enemy made no attempt to counter-attack; he retaliated slightly on ESSEX and WHITE TRENCHES during our bombardment, but heavily shelled and trench mortared EALING communication trench and LANCASHIRE FARM between 11-40 p.m. and midnight, but did not damage.

At midnight all was quiet.

One of the prisoners stated that the 86th Reserve Infantry Regiment left the SOMME on the 16th October and arrived here on the 25th October, he believes that the 84th Regiment are now on their right, but does not know who is on the left.

One of the prisoners also has the iron cross, which he states the KAISER presented to him at CAUDRY near CAMBRAI on the 17th instant. None were able to state what had happened to the 1st Guards Division.

(Sd) Arthur F. Smith,
Captain, G.S.,
for Brigadier-General,
Commanding 38th (Welsh) Division.

30/10/16.

WAR DIARY

FOR

NOVEMBER 1916

16th BATTALION

ROYAL WELSH FUSILIERS

WAR DIARY or INTELLIGENCE SUMMARY

Army Form C. 2118.

16th Bn. R.W.F.
113th Innf. Bde. 38th (Welsh) Division
VIII Corps

(Erase heading not required.)

Date	Summary of Events and Information	Remarks and references to Appendices
	Bn. in Front Line. Rgt. Protection - Platoon Formal.	
	Bn. relieved in Front Line. Eft. protection by 15th Bn. R.W.D. and	
	moved to Support engag. to CANAL BANK	
	Bn. in Support area. CANAL BANK.	
	Casualties 8th – 9th Drowned 1 O.R.	
	5 Reinforcements :- 35 O.R. from 4th Res. Bn. R.W.D.	
	6th " :- 38 O.R. "	
	7th " :- "	
	2/Lt. P.E. WILLIAMS joined the Bn. from Front Line. Gas Instruction.	
	Relieved 15th Bn. R.W.F. in Front Line. Gas Instruction.	
	Bn. in Front Line.	
	Casualties 10th – 13th :- NIL.	
9/10	Relieved in Front Line by 1st 11th Bn. P.W.B. 115th Inf. Bde.	
10th 13th	marched to D Camp - Divisional Reserve.	
13/6		

WAR DIARY
or
INTELLIGENCE SUMMARY

(Erase heading not required.)

Army Form C. 2118.

Date	Summary of Events and Information	Remarks and references to Appendices
	Divisional Reserve D Camp. Working parties (Cable Burying) supplied. Training & sundry fatigues.	
	Relieved 10th Bn. S.W.B. on CANAL BANK. Left Support Bn. Kept Position. Bn. in trenches at PESSELHOEK and on Traverses at YPRES ASYLUM	
	Relieved 11th Bn. S.W.B. in Front Line. Left position.	
	Bn. in Front Line	
	On night of 27th considerable enemy activity on our line — own Artillery retaliating. Very little damage from enemy bombardment.	
28th	Casualties 26th & 28th Wounded 2 O.R.	
28/29th	Bn. relieved in Front Line, left position by 15th Bn. R.W.F. & moved to Loggon Area on CANAL BANK	
29th 30th	Bn. in Support Area on CANAL BANK	

A.G. Pres Lieut. Col.
Commanding 16th Bn. R.W.F.

16th Battn: Royal Welsh Fusiliers

War Diary for December 1916.

Army Form C. 2118.

WAR DIARY
or
INTELLIGENCE SUMMARY

(Erase heading not required.)

16th Battalion R. Fusiliers
113th Inf. Brigade
38th (Welsh) Division

Instructions regarding War Diaries and Intelligence Summaries are contained in F. S. Regs., Part II. and the Staff Manual respectively. Title Pages will be prepared in manuscript.

Place	Date	Hour	Summary of Events and Information	Remarks and references to Appendices
Left Subsector	Dec 1st	—	Relieved 15th Bn R.Fusiliers in front line - Left Subsector. At 12 midnight intermittent hostile artillery activity on our trenches, which continued until 1 A.M. - Our artillery retaliating. At 12.10 a.m. enemy raid party entered our trenches. Enemy relieved the ? stay of only a few minutes. Casualties:- 1st M.G. Missing - Lt. P.A. Roberts, 1 O.R. Killed - 3 O.R. Wounded - 7 O.R.	
"	4th	—	Battalion relieved in front line by 15th Bn R.Fus. and moved to support dugouts on W bank of Canal. Casualties:- Killed 1 O.R. " - 6th Wounded 2 O.R.	
"	6th	—	Relieved 15th Bn R.Fusiliers in front line - Lillie Lion Corner. Casualties:- NIL. 6th - 9th	

Army Form C. 2118.

WAR DIARY
INTELLIGENCE SUMMARY
(Erase heading not required.)

Instructions regarding War Diaries and Intelligence Summaries are contained in F.S. Regs., Part II. and the Staff Manual respectively. Title Pages will be prepared in manuscript.

Place	Date	Hour	Summary of Events and Information	Remarks and references to Appendices
Left Sector	9th		Battalion relieved in front line by 13th Bn. R.W. Fusiliers, and moved to support dugouts W bank of Canal	
"	12th		Battalion relieved in support dugouts on W bank of Canal by 16th 16th Bn. Rifle Brigade. Battn en route at YPRES ASYLUM about 8.30 P.M. and arrived at POPERINGHE, where Battn. was billeted until the morning of 13th Dec.	
	13th		Battalion entrained at POPERINGHE at 10 A.M. and detrained at BOLLEZEELE - marched from BOLLEZEELE to billeting area (VOLCKERINGHOVE)	
	13th to 30th		Divisional Rest. – Battn in VOLCKERINGHOVE Training as per 113" Inf. Bde. programme	
			Reinforcements:-	
	14th		33 O.R.	
	15th		69 O.R.	
	25th		12 O.R.	
	30th		Battalion entrained at BOLLEZEELE and detrained at POPERINGHE – POPERINGHE to Camp "P". Battn in Camp "P". Telegrams	
	30 & 31		Nocturnal Recce. Battn in Camp "P". Bathing parties arranged	

I.V. Nunkin Major
Commanding 15th Battn.

WAR DIARY
FOR
JANUARY 1917.

95/14

16TH BATT: ROYAL WELSH FUSILIERS.

Army Form C. 2118.

WAR DIARY
or
INTELLIGENCE SUMMARY
(Erase heading not required.)

16th Bn. Rl Fusiliers
113th Inf. Brigade
38th (Welsh) Division

Instructions regarding War Diaries and Intelligence Summaries are contained in F.S. Regs., Part II and the Staff Manual respectively. Title Pages will be prepared in manuscript.

Place	Date	Hour	Summary of Events and Information	Remarks and references to Appendices
	1st/6 13th		Divisional Rest - Battalion in Camp "P". Training as per Bn. programme. Working and carrying parties supplied. Casualties :- Sick 5 O.R. Reinforcements 1st :- 10 O.R. 2nd :- 17 O.R. 10th :- 2 O.R. Reinforcement Officers 2/Lt E.D'Reca 2/Lt Neal 2/Lt Gething Capt J.A. Griffiths 2/Lt Eammons	
	13th 14th		Relieved 16th Bn. Rifle Brigade in Support Area on W. of CANAL BANK - Left Subsection. Relieved 17th Bn. K.R.R's in front line - Rene subsection. Situation - Very Quiet. Casualties :- Killed 2 O.R. 14th & 18th Wounded 1 O.R. Reinforcement Officers :- 2/Lt Jarclough & 17th 2/Lt J.C. Morris	
	18th		Relieved in front line by 15th Bn. Rl Fus., & moved to Support area on W. of CANAL BANK. Casualties :- Wounded 4 O.R. 18th & 22nd Sick 3 O.R. Reinforcement Officers :- 2/Lt V.P. Williams & 20th 2/Lt G. Williams & 20th	

Army Form C. 2118.

WAR DIARY
or
INTELLIGENCE SUMMARY
(Erase heading not required.)

16th Bn. R. W. Fus.
113 Inf. Brigade
38th (Welsh) Division

Place	Date	Hour	Summary of Events and Information	Remarks and references to Appendices
	22nd		On the Afternoon of 20 Many unusual enemy artillery activity on CANAL BANK lasting about 15 mins - our artillery retaliating. Casualties in O.R. Relieved 15th Bn R.W.Fus in front line. Casualties :- 22nd to 26th Situation - Very Quiet	
	24th		Sent 2 O.P. Relieved in trenches C.13.3 and C.13.2 L.Rly Trench Mgo Lancashire Farm Section) by 13th Bn R.W.Fus. Post on SKIPTON ROAD taken over from 14th Bn R.W.Fus	
	26th		Batt. relieved in front line by the 13th Bn R.W.Fusiliers, and moved to Support Area on W of CANAL BANK. One company moved to POPERINGHE for Baths + Rest - entraining at YPRES ASYLUM and detraining at POPERINGHE.	
	28th		The company at POPERINGHE returned to Support Area on W of CANAL BANK Casualties :- Sent 4 O.P. 26th to 30th	
	30th		Relieved 15th Bn. R.W.Fus in front line. Casualties :- NIL. Situation :- Normal 30th to 31st	

[signature]
Lt-Col.
Commanding 16th Bn. R.W.Fus

WAR DIARY
16th BATTN. D.W.F.

FEBRUARY 1917

WAR DIARY or INTELLIGENCE SUMMARY

Army Form C. 2118.

16th Bn Royal Welsh Fusiliers
113th Inf Bde
38th (Welsh) Division

Place	Date	Hour	Summary of Events and Information	Remarks and references to Appendices
February 1916	2nd		Battn in front line - Regt Instruction	
			1st Enemy Activity: Enemy shelled COLNE VALLEY and WHITE TRENCH with shells of light calibre. 9:25? Shot 1 dud m.i. shells. 10–10:45am Our Artillery retaliating. The CO on CANAL was broken by the R.E. in conjunction with Battn. Workers opposite C.F.35 v FARGATE STRONG POINT. Trenches from HUDDLESTON to C.132 under water everywhere – Light north easterly.	
			2nd Enemy retaliating the organised shelling of German line opposite BOESINGHE, but most of this was to the left of our frontage. Enemy trench-mortars active on our left company from 3:40am to 5:15am. Our Artillery replied but an organised bombardment on Enemy's line all day.	
			3rd At 7am Enemy opened out a sharp bombardment on our trenches between HUDDLESTON ROAD and Bttn 18. Enemy T.M's active on our left company front from 4am – 5:30am. Enemy M.Guns more active than usual. Our Artillery active at intervals all day especially 1:30–2:30am & 11:30am. Relay system of Runners posted at 8pm & Wire from 7:30 – 11pm.	
			A daylight patrol of 1 Offr & 9 O.R. went out last night. Enemy wire from CAESAR'S NOSE to The left inspected, but no gaps reported.	
			WORK: 1 Offr & 3 men went to the new trench at Bttn 22. Wiring in front of Bttn 22 & repairing Bttn 19 & 20.	
			Casualties: Sick 3.	
	3/4/5		Battn relieved in front line by the 15th Bn Welsh & moved to support area on W.B. of CANAL BANK. One company detached to POPERINGHE and another to W.CANAL BANK.	
	4/6		The CO on CANAL was broken nightly in conjunction with 151 R.E's. Wiring Iron Bridge and Passage GD. Iron bath at flying point. Ammunition at C.32; GHQ on FARGATE: Dug-outs near Bttn 22 and Reserve Posn in BARNSLEY POST. Carrying parties supplied for emergencies supplies at	

WAR DIARY

Army Form C. 2118.

(Erase heading not required.)
(2)

Place	Date	Hour	Summary of Events and Information	Remarks and references to Appendices
	7/8/13		Batt: 18 x ESSEX. Batty went to Ringrose on YPRES LEE BANK.	
			Casualties 1. Died of Wounds Reinforcements to 2/Lt C.J. HEARTLEY	
			4 to 7th 2. Wounded " W.T. WILLIAMS joined Battn 6.2.17	
			1. Sick " N. HARPER	
	8th 6		Batt. relieved the 13th Bn Bedfs in front line	
			8th Exceptionally quiet day	
			Wiring from MIDDLETON FORD to E.27 continued	
	9th		Enemy activity:- generally quiet. Our artillery ¼ element.	
			But our own behind enemy line to the left of CAESAR'S NOSE in early afternoon	
			Wiring from MIDDLETON FORD to E.27 completed	
	10th		Operations:- East Riding Raid	
			A small enemy working party observed at 5.45 A.M. to 10 night of PLUSH FARM.	
			They appeared to be wiring, but are not remain long.	
	1/11		Few observed movement observed at C.M.A. movement observed at about C.B.27.E	
			A Sniping Patrol was out nightly when in front line. Enemy flares were seeing at	
			C.7.C.8.9 & 7.nexts the shelling of ridge lines behind the enemy lines at C7.C.10.5	
			Bruised trenches were renewed immediately before our with wire leading	
			Parallel to CANAL BANK	
			11 Patrols B/N.C.O.+ 2 men went out nightly to observe the enemy wire and to	
			ascertain if enemy was forming up in No mans land. No enemy movement was	
			observed	
			Daily Returns as per reports produced	
			Casualties Sick N.C.R.	
			8th 6 11th	
	11/12		Battn. relieved in front line by the 15th Bn Bedfs and moved to support area on W of	
			CANAL BANK	

WAR DIARY or INTELLIGENCE SUMMARY

Army Form C. 2118.

Place	Date	Hour	Summary of Events and Information	Remarks and references to Appendices
	12th/6 15th		The Company proceeded to POPERINGHE on training at YPRES ASYLUM. Returned to in CANAL BANK 14.2.17. Work continued on Aug. 16th & 17th Batt 23; Bty H.Q. in FARGATE TRENCH & Firing Point at 532. Daily work in YPRES Aug. 17.	
	12th 6		Enemy carried out a sharp bombardment on the evening along CANAL BANK. Training carried out as per reports herewith. Casualties 12th 6. 13th — 1 O.R. killed, 5 sick	
	15/16/3		Relieved the 18th A. Bn. Res. in front line.	
	16th 6 19th		Observation. Enemy artillery fairly quiet in the 6th sector & machine guns normal. Went on trenches during the night. At 10 p.m. enemy sent to about 30 + H.Q. 77mm shells to the right of CLUNE VALLEY — dropping in neighbourhood of CORRIDOR TRENCH. Killing 1 O.R. about 10 minutes	
	17th		Enemy sent few W.W. shells into station on CANAL BANK at 5:20 p.m. Extremely quiet day and entire absence of enemy machine guns on our lk.	
	18th		Enemy artillery very quiet during 15 day & on the absence of enemy artillery and machine guns fire on the enemy. Enemy retaliation to our bombardment 3.30 a.m. but did very little damage. Our own was broken and there types C.72 & C.74. Dugout Post at C.70 was damaged in by 18 pounders. The trench was damaged as per report – C.75 cleared out.	
	19th		Enemy shelled CANAL BANK with heavy shells and shrapnel from 1 a.m. – 1:30 a.m. Telephone communications to Liaison Bde H.Q. and Coys cut off. Police went out nightly. Training carried out as per reports herewith. Casualties: Bde J.Osman 1 O.R., Casualties 2 O.R., 18th 6. 19th 2 O.R.	

2449 Wt. W14957/Mgo 750,000 1/16 J.B.C. & A. Forms/C.2118/12.

WAR DIARY or INTELLIGENCE SUMMARY

Army Form C. 2118.

Instructions regarding War Diaries and Intelligence Summaries are contained in F. S. Regs., Part II. and the Staff Manual respectively. Title Pages will be prepared in manuscript.

(Erase heading not required.)

Place	Date	Hour	Summary of Events and Information	Remarks and references to Appendices
	19/7/20		Relieved in front line by the 15th Bn. R.W.Fus — The company proceeded to POPERINGHE and returned on 21st	
	20th to 23rd		Work done:- (1) Continuation of different Ref. at junction of HUDDLESTON ROAD & CORNWALLIS.	
			(2) Work on Strong Point at S.32.	
			(3) Work on Coy H.Q. at OLD ARGATE, Bart 22.	
			(4) Commenced work on new Battle dug-out near G.S. Bridge	
			(5) Wiring round No 1 Reserve Posn - completing & check	
	Casualties 20th to 23rd			
			Relieved 15th Bn. R.W.Fus on front line	
	24th		Very quiet	
	25th		Enemy bombardment 2.5.0 am to 2.35 am on Batt 17. 3 am to 3.30 am retaliation in reply to hostile bombardment	
			Enemy TMs registering near HUDDLESTON X ROADS during morning & aft	
			Reported attacks of enemy trench mor. Inc fire from approx. at C.13.6.9.5.9.	
			A rapid firing enemy Machine Gun from Sapo at C.7.d.9.2.	
			Batt 17 was arrived by enemy bombardment.	
	26th		A number of tin pots were seen to be raised & lowered at entrance point to certain German front line	
	27th		Enemy Machine Gun active from CAESAR'S NOSE Nr. Regnir Posn 1.2.3.	
			Our Artillery violently bombarded enemy trenches during morning and afternoon. Large quantities of earth thrown up about C.14.a.	
			Wiring :- On Coys & Spor B wiring round No 1 Regnir Posn.	
			Training :- no fire reports received	Kellie S. O.P. Wormwit 1. O.R. Regnal Lin 24th to 27th

Army Form C. 2118.

WAR DIARY
or
INTELLIGENCE SUMMARY

(Erase heading not required.)

Instructions regarding War Diaries and Intelligence Summaries are contained in F. S. Regs., Part II. and the Staff Manual respectively. Title Pages will be prepared in manuscript.

Place	Date	Hour	Summary of Events and Information	Remarks and references to Appendices
	27/28		Relieved in front line by 15th Bn. RifBde.	
	28th		Continuation of work 20th to 23rd. Situation very quiet.	

A.G. Jones
Lt. Col.
Commanding 16th Bn. RifBde.

16th BATT. ROYAL WELSH FUSILIERS Vol/6

WAR DIARY

FOR

MARCH 1917.

WAR DIARY

16th Battn. R. W. Fusiliers.
113th Inf. Brigade.
38th (Welsh) Divn.

INTELLIGENCE SUMMARY
(1)

Army Form C. 2118.

Place	Date	Hour	Summary of Events and Information	Remarks and references to Appendices
Left Subsector	1st & 3rd		Battn. in Support Area on W. Canal Bank.	
			Work done:- Continuation of work on Strong Point at S.32; Continuation of work on Coy.H.Q. at Old Fargate and Butt 22; Continuation of work on New Battle Dug-out near Bridge 6B; Wiring round No2 Picquet Post - 48 coils wire put out.	
	3/4th		Relieved the 15th Battn.R.W.F. in front line -Left Subsection.	
			4th. Movement observed at C.8.a.2.4. at 7.45.a.m. but light and visibility too poor to see clearly.	
			9.a.m. Enemy wiring in vicinity of PILCKEM (approx. C.2.c.8.1.) Artillery notified and party dispersed when fired at.	
			Reinforcements :- 2/Lt. W.H.JONES joined Battalion.	
			5th. Small hostile party filed overland from approx. C.7.c.9.1. to C.7.d.1.8. when they disappeared into trench at 8.45.a.m. - Two of enemy appeared to be digging at C.8.a.2.2. at 3.45.p.m.	
			6th. Enemy T.M's active on Right Battn. Front 3 - 4.p.m. 5.p.m. enemy shelled W-Canal Bank near 6W Bridge. 4 - 5.30.p.m. enemy aeroplanes active.	
			3-4.p.m. Our Artillery retaliating. Our T.M's and Stokes retaliating for enemy T.M's from 3-4.p.m.	
			7th. 12.15.p.m. Enemy Artillery registered with four Whizzbangs on the screen fixed on trees on BOESINGHE-YPRES Road at B.18.d.6.0.	
			8.50-9.p.m. Enemy again shelled the above screen.	
			9.10.a.m. Smoke observed rising from German Trenches at C.2.c.7.3.	
			A Fighting Patrol of 1 Off. & 9 O.R. went out nightly. On morning of 4th. enemy patrol met near their own wire & drove them in. Shots were fired and bombs thrown on both sides. Casualties:- 1 O.R. slightly wounded.	
"	7/8th		The Battn. relieved in front line by the 15th Battn. R.W.F. and moved to Support dug-outs on W Canal Bank.	
			8th to 10th. Work done:- Continuation of work on Coy H.Q. at Welsh Harp and Flash Alley; Continuation on Strong Point at S.32; Completion of Defense Post at Huddleston Road.	
"	10/11th		Battn. relieved the 15th Battn. R.W.F. in front line.	

WAR DIARY
or
INTELLIGENCE SUMMARY.
(Erase heading not required.)

Army Form C. 2118.

Place	Date	Hour	Summary of Events and Information	Remarks and references to Appendices
Lft. Subsector			11th. Enemy shelled screen on YPRES-BOESINGHE Road about B.18.d.6.1. during the evening. Hostile aeroplanes very active especially between 11.a.m. & noon. Sign of work in progress observed at C.7.d.7.6. - one of enemy seen for a few minutes working on parapet.	
			12th. Enemy activity:- Very quiet; Our activity:- Active at intervals otherwise quiet. Hostile shells (probably 5.9") between screen at B.18.d. and Canal Bank from Bridge 6B to 6D -11.30.a.m. to 12.30.p.m.	
			Enemy shelling of screen at B.18.d. repeated at 8.45.p.m. and retaliation was asked for and some forty rounds were fired on enemy lines.	
			3.55.p.m. Conflagration seen from Battn. H.Q. C.13.c.1½.1 (Bridge 6W) at bearing 59.	
			13th. 5.p.m. Hostile shells (4.2" or 5.9") were fired from direction of ARTILLERY WOOD. Three blind shells fell in No Man's Land near Post 8 (C.7.1 to C.7.2.) Several shells dropped between that post and Fargate Strong Point, and one between Fargate Strong Point and the protecting wire.	
			8.50.a.m. Suspicious movement going on approx. C.2.d.2.2.. An object having the appearance of a large black square was observed swaying to and fro and occasionally disappearing from view. Object again seen at 3.50.p.m.	
			14th. 8.30.p.m. Enemy reported to have bombed his own wire opposite Post 8. (C.7.1. to C.7.2.)	
			Reinforcements :- 2/Lt. W.O.HUGHES joined Battalion.	
			12.15 to 12.30.p.m. Our artillery opened rapid fire on enemy line about C.14.a. 12.10.p.m. One of enemy seen moving along trench at CAESAR'S NOSE.	
			Fighting Patrol of 1 Off. & 9 O.R. sent out nightly; Casualties; 1 O.R. Slightly Wounded.	
	14/15		Battalion relieved in front line by 13th Battn. R.W.F. 15th to 18th. Battn. in Support Dug-outs on W Canal Bank Continuation of work as for 8th to 10th.	
	18/19		Relieved 13th Battn. R.W.F. in front line	

Army Form C. 2118.

WAR DIARY
or
INTELLIGENCE SUMMARY. (3)
(Erase heading not required.)

Instructions regarding War Diaries and Intelligence Summaries are contained in F. S. Regs., Part II, and the Staff Manual respectively. Title pages will be prepared in manuscript.

Place	Date	Hour	Summary of Events and Information	Remarks and references to Appendices
	19th.		Smoke seen issuing from enemy lines along the edge of ARTILLERY WOOD at 12.25.p.m.	
	20th.		Our Artillery fairly active during the day. Fighting Patrol of 1 Off. & 9 O.R. went out nightly. Casualties:- 1 O.R. Wounded.	
			Battalion relieved in front line by the 17th Battn. R.W.Fus. - Battalion entrained at YPRES ASYLUM at 12.30.a.m. (22nd) and detrained at ESQUELBECQ - March from ESQUELBECQ to BOLLEZEELE (Billeting Area)	
31st March/ 1st April	22nd. to 31st.		Divisional Reserve. Training carried out as per programmes rendered.	
			Battalion moved from BOLLEZEELE to E Canal Bank - Left Reserve Position - Right Bde. Relieved 13th Battalion R.W.Fusiliers.	
	24th.		Reinforcements :- 2/Lt. W.S.GOFF.) Joined Battalion. 2/Lt. G.O.PARRY.)	

C. C. Potter
Lieut.Col.
Commanding 16th Battn. R.W.Fusiliers.

16th BATTN. ROYAL WELSH FUSILIERS.

WAR DIARY

FOR

APRIL 1917.

Army Form C. 2118.

WAR DIARY
or
INTELLIGENCE SUMMARY.

16th Bn R. Welsh Fusiliers
113th Inf Brigade
38th (Welsh) Division

(Erase heading not required.)

Place	Date	Hour	Summary of Events and Information	Remarks and references to Appendices
April 1917				
Left Sect.	1st 6		Bath in Left Recess Sector - Right Brigade	
Sector	4th		Work Order: (1) Work on Canal Bank Defences (2) Work on Coy. H.Q. at LANCASHIRE FARM, HEADINGLY and NIKE. (3) Work on HUDDERSFIELD Communication Trench between HUDDERSFIELD and NEW HALIFAX ROAD. Trench before Pot (?) Wiring. Training carried out daily as per reports rendered.	
			Casualties :- Sick 1 O.R.	
			1st 6 H.Q.	
"	4/6/17		Relieved 13th Bn R. Welsh Fusiliers in Front Line - Left Coy Right Brigade	
			Bn. H.Q. moved from R. Canal Bank to W. Canal Bank	
	5th	12-5 p.m.	Enemy shelled against LANCASHIRE FARM Road between R.E.'s and Front Line with H. 2" Shells.	
	6th		Artillery on both Sides fairly quiet. Enemy and our Machine Guns very active.	
			Enemy attempted to be heavily covering his new's offrs - his being accompanied by Enemy Machine Gun fire. Snipers seen hiding from enemy trenches at approximately	

WAR DIARY
or
INTELLIGENCE SUMMARY.
(Erase heading not required.)

Army Form C. 2118.

Place	Date	Hour	Summary of Events and Information	Remarks and references to Appendices
C.14.a.3.4.				
		5-10 p.m.	3rd Sp. 16 enemy were seen traversing a gap in his front line	
at C.14.a.3.4.				
	7th	At 12.30 a.m. our Lewis gun reports falling short by Left front Coy. 5.0 a.m. Shell falling in R Nile.		
			From Enemy Machine Guns very active during the night.	
			Casualties 5th to 8th Sick 1 O.R.	
	8/9th		Bn relieved in Front line by the 13th Bn Middlesex and moved to Left Reserve Position. Bn. H.Q. moved from W. CANAL BANK to E CANAL BANK	
	9th-11th		Continuation of work as for 1st to 6th inst. Training carried out daily as per reports rendered	
			Casualties: Killed 3 O.R. Sick 2 O.R.	
	11/12th		Bn relieved in Left Reserve Position - Right Brigade by the 14th Bn Welsh Regiment. Bn moved to Camp "E" (A.30)	
	12th 12 noon		Divisional Reserve - Bn in "E" Camp.	

WAR DIARY
or
INTELLIGENCE SUMMARY.
(Erase heading not required.)

Army Form C. 2118.

(3)

Place	Date	Hour	Summary of Events and Information	Remarks and references to Appendices
	17th		Col. F.N. WILLIAMS assumed command with the Military Medal by the Brig.- Gen. Comdg. Reviewed 12th March 1917	
			Training was carried out daily as per training programme	
			Inspired	
			Casualties Sick H.O.R.	
	22/23rd		The Bn. relieved the 10th Bn. Welsh Regiment in Right Front Sector (LANCASHIRE FARM)	
	23rd		Enemy artillery shot over shells to various points in our line — Our artillery retaliated on enemy by sending a reply fire etc.	
			KRUPP SALIENT. 9.15 a.m. Smoke seen rising from enemy front line at approx. C.14.a.M.3.	
		12.40 p.m	Enemy seen moving in his front line trench at C.14.a.M.3. but did not appear to be working.	
			Small amount of wire netting on 15th Division during 15 day. Sniping reported enemy working hard at a point L of VON KLUCK COT. C.14.K.H.2. from 6am to 10am each morning. Artillery notified	

WAR DIARY or INTELLIGENCE SUMMARY

Army Form C. 2118.

(Erase heading not required.)

Place	Date	Hour	Summary of Events and Information	Remarks and references to Appendices
			and fire opened. This work is very conspicuous — is covering of	
			Lombartzyde new thing with sheet nickels and stones well above the earth	
			parapet. It seems too neat to me.	
			2AB Enemy working party near VON KLUCK COT. Machinegun activities at	
			"Stein Busch". Much land hammering was heard. Three times fired on	
			15 junction of the water, which ceased.	
			Enemy TM's retaliated for our bombardment. We opened with Rifle	
			Grenades on Pat 21 (C.14.C.H.92), his employed Minenwerfer on our	
			Luking on the parapet on Pat 19 (C.14.C.7.7). To remember trenches	
			active.	
			Our Artillery very active throughout the afternoon (from 2-6 p.m.).	
			Shells heard falling in enemy wire and trench at KRUPP SALIENT.	
			Considerable aerial activity throughout the day on both sides, and	
			Ant. Aircraft guns displayed considerable activity.	
			10.70 pm. Enemy opened a heavy bombardment on the right,	
			which spread along our front. Rifle & machine guns and SOS were seen	

WAR DIARY
or
INTELLIGENCE SUMMARY.
(Erase heading not required.)

Army Form C. 2118.

(5)

Place	Date	Hour	Summary of Events and Information	Remarks and references to Appendices

going up on the right, which appeared to be ours. This was followed by a Red light from our Right Coy front, another Red soon after from Right Coy front – another from Support trench LANCASHIRE FARM and from CANAL BANK. Our artillery answered 15 enemy's S.O.S. promptly and heavily and enemy's bombardment died down at 10.30 p.m.

25th. Our artillery shelled enemy line at intervals all morning. Fire increasing slightly in intensity during the afternoon. Our T.M's active during the afternoon – shells falling on enemy line near KRUPP SALIENT. As a result of our bombardment on enemy's line – enemy wire was cut at C.14.c.7.2.95 leaving a gap of about 20 yds. At C.14.a.7.3 this is a big gap in enemy (?inch). Enemy seen mending 15 gap in 15 mornings and sniper had some kills.

Between 6.45 p.m. and 7.15 p.m. the (?Howitzer) were firing short in front of Right front Coy. Battery concerned was warned and

Army Form C. 2118.

WAR DIARY
or
INTELLIGENCE SUMMARY.
(Erase heading not required.)

Place	Date	Hour	Summary of Events and Information	Remarks and references to Appendices
			Firing ceased.	
	26/6		Enemy wiring party reported at C.14.c.75.95. Our Lewis Guns fired with burst during the night.	
			Training was carried out daily as per reports attached.	
			Casualties 23rd 26th Killed 1 O.R. Wounded 1 O.R.	
	26/27		Bn relieved in front line by the 13th Bn R28 Div. Bn H.Q. moved from W Canal Bank to E. Canal Bank.	
	27/6		Batln in Support area 6th E. CANAL BANK.	
	30th		Training carried out daily.	
			Reinforcements:- 2/Lt W.H. JONES } Joined Batln 27-11-17 2/Lt A.E. INGLIS }	
			29th 37683 Pte T. AGAIN evacuated with R. Military fever by 12 Brig. Gen. Hosp. Evacuated 28/4/17.	
			Received 13 Bn R28Div in front line.	
Second 1st May				

A. J. Scott
Lt. Col.
Commanding 16th Bn R28 Div.

16th ROYAL WELSH FUSILIERS Vol 18

WAR DIARY

FOR

MAY 19/17

18 F
7 sheets

Army Form C. 2118.

6th Bn R Dunkles
113 Inf Brigade
38th (Welsh) Divn

WAR DIARY
INTELLIGENCE SUMMARY.
(Erase heading not required.)

Instructions regarding War Diaries and Intelligence Summaries are contained in F.S. Regs., Part II. and the Staff Manual respectively. Title pages will be prepared in manuscript.

Place	Date	Hour	Summary of Events and Information	Remarks and references to Appendices
Right Sub-Section	13/6		Bn in Front Line - Right Sector - Right Brigade	
(YPRES FARM)	14th	1st	At 1am enemy artillery opened a bombardment at 1.0am to Germans SOS signals were sent up and was immediately answered by the German batteries and Minenwerfers. Enemy barrage was Mining of 8", 5.9" and Minenwerfers. The salient from SKIPTON on to an YPRES FARM which gradually lengthened on each side of HUDDERSFIELD TRENCH. The enemy retaliation was feeble and barrage very irregular. Enemy ceased fire at 2am. German SOS signal appeared to be Green. After early morning bombardment enemy trenches have been watched in enemy trenches at C.14.a. Enemy being much reported at C.14.a.9.3. (approx). Smoke issuing from behind CAESAR'S NOSE at 7.50am - Movement noticed at KRUPP SALIENT at 9.55am - Considerable shell activity during the morning.	

WAR DIARY
or
INTELLIGENCE SUMMARY.
(Erase heading not required.)

Army Form C. 2118.

Instructions regarding War Diaries and Intelligence Summaries are contained in F. S. Regs., Part II. and the Staff Manual respectively. Title pages will be prepared in manuscript.

Place	Date	Hour	Summary of Events and Information	Remarks and references to Appendices
	2nd		Our artillery fairly active during the day – Slightly shelling the rear of enemy lines during the afternoon. Shells falling in vicinity of KOHN FARM. Enemy seen moving in line trench at C.1.a.6.2. and near KRUPP SALIENT. Tac account of cloud activity during the morning our Gunners kept silence. Our artillery opened fire on enemy at 10.15 p.m. on reports of Gas alarm. Our guns reported fire firing short by Bd.21 (C.M.C.S.B) – his falling no 400 to front of Bd.21 – word sent into it.	
	3rd		Our artillery shelled the rear of the enemy's line at intervals throughout the day. Some observed to have with considerable effect on enemy trench in the vicinity of ESSEN FARM at about 6.15 p.m. Considerable artillery activity on our side. Engagement to both sides. Towards the afternoon enemy planes reported approaching our lines in the afternoon enemy M.G. fire throughout the night	
	4th		Everything quiet except for considerable	

WAR DIARY or INTELLIGENCE SUMMARY

Army Form C. 2118.

(Erase heading not required.)

Place	Date	Hour	Summary of Events and Information	Remarks and references to Appendices
			A party of enemy seen working in the gaps of the wire. Which at	
			0.1 H. A.7.0. Party disturbed by Lewis Gun fire.	
			Night:- Wiring HQrs in front of SKIPTON and Gals 16-21.	
			2nd Patrol. Fighting Patrol sent out Bn 1/2nd & 2/3rd. Nothing to report	
	4/5²		Relieved in front line by the 13th Bn. R.W.Fus. Bn HQ moved from	
			N. Canal Bank to E. Canal Bank.	
			Work NR.: (i) 17oft Dr Coy HQ on DYKE (ii) Reclamation of Bogus line & Trenches	
			3ʳᵈ & 5ᵗʰ. PIXNEM RD AND SKIPTON (iii) Reclamation of & line Sandbagging	
			HALIFAX TRENCH (iv) Cable burying	
			Training carried out daily as per reports rendered	
	8/9²		Relieved the 13th Bn R.W.Fus in front line - Bn HQ moved from E. Canal Bank	
			to N. Canal Bank	
		9⁵	Our artillery shelled various parts of German line - 5pm Shelling	
			near HIGH COMMAND REDOUBT; otherwise nothing unusual happened.	
		10²	Enemy artillery fairly active at intervals between 7.30 am &	
			11.30 am. Our artillery retaliated on enemy line (C.W.S.)	

WAR DIARY or INTELLIGENCE SUMMARY

Army Form C. 2118.

(Erase heading not required.)

Place	Date	Hour	Summary of Events and Information	Remarks and references to Appendices

also Sr. KRUPP SALIENT.
Considerable aerial activity during the morning.

1/A Enemy shelled SKIPTON RD & near PO Front line with 77mm.
Minenwerfers also sent over Post 25, which was badly damaged.
Our artillery active between 12.10 P.m. & 12.40 P.m. - Heavy fire.
Pt. 25mm C114.a.2.8.
Considerable amount of aerial activity. 8.25 a.m. Enemy plane over our lines, but driven back by Anti-Aircraft Guns, also fired on by Machine Guns.
Enemy appears to be repairing the Front line to the left of KRUPP SALIENT & a considerable exhibit. A good quantity of backward movement has been seen.

Wiring Thickening of entanglements & filling up gaps at C.14.D-C.14.10
9"d 2" & left front of Pot 25" in the night.
Pol'ite 819" Reconnoitering Patrol. 2/10", 10/11", 11/12" Daylight Patrols
9" & 12" to Enemy encroachment. Enemy opened fire on Patrol.
Casual times:
nyt 10/11" when returning. 1 wounded.
2/Lt V.C. MORRIS.

Bn. relieved in front line by R Btln B.Dn.-

17/13"

WAR DIARY or INTELLIGENCE SUMMARY

Army Form C. 2118.

(Erase heading not required.)

Place	Date	Hour	Summary of Events and Information	Remarks and references to Appendices
Noordhoek				
	13th-16th		Continuation in the 5th & 8th	
16/17th			Relieved 18th Bn. R.S. Bn. in front line. Bn. H.Q. moved from E. Canal Bank to W. Canal Bank.	
	17th		Big fire reported behind enemy lines opposite SKIPTON - reserve Ammunition Dump.	
			Wiring & strengthening wire in front and to right of Pat. 23, and filling gaps in front of posts 16-21.	
	18th 19th			
	Patrols	1617th, 1718th	Daylight Patrols went out - No enemy snipers fired	
	17th-19th			
19/20th			Bn. relieved in front line by R. 15th Bn. West Regiment - Bn. moved to Dugout area on E. Canal Bank.	
			2nd Relief Relieved in Dugout Posts by 16. 10th Bn. West Regiment	
			Bn. entrained at YPRES ASYLUM and detrained at POPERINGHE - march from POPERINGHE to "Y" Camp, where billeted for the night.	
	20th		Bn. marched from "Y" Camp to HERZEELE	
	20th - 30th		Corps Reserve - Bn. billeted in HERZEELE. Training carried out as per programme enclosed.	
	30th		Bn. marched from HERZEELE to BUYSSCHEURE (Billeting area)	

Vol 19

19 F
5 sheets

16½ BATT ROYAL WELSH FUSILIERS

WAR DIARY

FOR

JUNE 1917

WAR DIARY / INTELLIGENCE SUMMARY

Army Form C. 2118.

16th Bn. R.W.Fus.
113 Inf. Brigade
38th Divn.

June 1917

Place	Date	Hour	Summary of Events and Information	Remarks and references to Appendices
	1st/6th		— Corps Review —	
	10th		Battalion in Training at QUEENS AREA — killed in SETQUES. Training carried out as per programme reviewed. On 10th June the Battalion in conjunction with 14th Bn. R.W.Fus carried out an approach march to enemy positions preparatory to an attack, and a subsequent advance in attack formation.	
			Our demonstration was carried out in conjunction with above Scheme.	
		3.0	Sgt. T. Edwards awarded the D.C.M. for services in the field	
		10.0	Battalion moved to "X" Camp — Entrained at ST OMER at 4:40 p.m. and detrained at POPERINGHE at 7:30 p.m. — March from POPERINGHE to Camp	
		12.0	Reinforcements of 67 ORs from 3rd Bn. R.W.Fus.	
	12th/13th		Battn. relieved the 13th Bn. R.W.Fus. in Right Reserve position (LA'SHIRE FARM SECTOR) (ST JULIEN, 28 NW.)	
			Battn. on trained at POPERINGHE, and detrained at H.10.b — (sheet 4) progress marching to the following casualties. CANAL BANK — Batt. coln. was heavily shelled when relief was in progress resulting in the following casualties :—	

Killed 2/Lt. E. D. REES.
Wounded 2/Lt. F.C.H. EDWARDSON

8 O.Rs
15 men etc.

WAR DIARY
or
INTELLIGENCE SUMMARY.

Army Form C. 2118.

(continued)

Place	Date	Hour	Summary of Events and Information	Remarks and references to Appendices
	14/15ᵗʰ		39ᵗʰ Division left over a portion of the 113ᵗʰ Inf Brigade front, and "A" + "B" Coys moved into Bivouacs in L.2. Work on the Wood and B.23 (ST JULIEN 28 N.W.2) Communication Trenches continued. Huts 303, Kitchener's Wood, "C" and "D" Coys and HQrs moved in above.	
	15/16ᵗʰ		16ᵗʰ – 28ᵗʰ Battalion in Bivouac. Battalion was employed during the nights on various working parties — chiefly trench digging. Work Done: Skipton Communication Trench on Skipton Exterior (on) M.G. Emplacements (work carried out on the Front rendered)	
			16ᵗʰ Road due E of Wood B.23 Shelled at 8.30pm	
			18ᵗʰ B.23 (Drived) during the day up to 10-30pm when Light Railway running parallel to BRIELEN–ELVERDINGHE ROAD was Shelled at intervals up to 7pm. Shells falling short of Railway + 400 yds. D.W. of Wood.	
			3 a.m. Heavy shelling of DAWSON'S CORNER	
	19ᵗʰ		Working party at SKIPTON hampered by shelling to some extent – that of the Shells going over the Trench	
			B.23. 2am – 3am. Several enemy Shells fell almost on the W edge of the Wood.	

WAR DIARY
or
INTELLIGENCE SUMMARY.
(Erase heading not required.)

Army Form C. 2118.

Instructions regarding War Diaries and Intelligence Summaries are contained in F. S. Regs., Part II. and the Staff Manual respectively. Title pages will be prepared in manuscript. (continued)

Place	Date	Hour	Summary of Events and Information	Remarks and references to Appendices
		10.3	Reinforcements:- 5 H ORs from 3rd Bn. Bedfs.	
	21st	11.23.	Shelling of road running along N. edge of Wood from DAWSON'S CORNER with M.2. shells. Enemy Shelling back-area – Counter Battery work. Several enemy aeroplanes over back area early in the morning – flying low.	
		22.70	10.30 a.m. Enemy shelled NAVARA FARM & the edge of the Wood. Reinforcements:- 67 ORs from 6th Kent and 16 Cheshire Regt. The Enemy's attention was actively drawn to by a working party.	
		24.42	Col. R.T. McGAIR announces to M.M. the services in the Field.	
		25.28	Shelling of road running along the edge of wood from DAWSON'S CORNER (at intervals)	
	26/27th		Enemy aeroplane flew back area about 9.00 p.m. Driven back by A.A. Guns. A raid was carried out by a party of 1 Off. & 16 ORs. The aim was a silent one as regards Artillery fire, but was assisted by overhead M.G. fire. The party advanced in No Man's Land and officer led an entry into the Enemy's line without the Enemy becoming aware of it, at C.I.H.a. 3. 2. 7. (ST JULIEN 28.N.W.2) at 12.55 a.m. A party of the Enemy was encountered and party (number in enemy team & Coys not known). A Coy SS men (probably 20 or 30) advanced from a Sap. The raiding party responded in reply. The enemy retreated over the top firing from the Support trench to our G. attack over the top firing from the Volunteer troops & their interactions – NIL at 1.10 a.m. Identifications: - NIL.	

WAR DIARY
or
INTELLIGENCE SUMMARY.

(Erase heading not required.)

Army Form C. 2118.

(Continued).

Place	Date	Hour	Summary of Events and Information	Remarks and references to Appendices
	28ᵗʰ		Casualties Killed - 2/Lt Wm Hugh Jones. " ORs :- 7 Wounded ORs - 40.	
	29ᵗʰ		Battn. relieved by the 2ⁿᵈ Battn. S.W.B. and moved by march route to Transport Lines. Major H.D.N. Fourdrin with one Company of Battn. via L.de.V. & Loves Battn. moved by Molo Bureau to CASTRE, and on the following day to REZ.	
	30ᵗʰ		Reinforcements :- 44 ORs from 6ᵗʰ Cheshire Regiment	

J.H. Jourdain Maj.
O.C. 16ᵗʰ Bn. R.Fusiliers

16TH BN ROYAL WELSH FUSILIERS

WAR DIARY

JULY – 1917

WAR DIARY or INTELLIGENCE SUMMARY

Army Form C. 2118.

16th Batt. Rif. Fusiliers
1/3rd ... Bde
30th (Notts) Division

Month: JULY

Place	Date	Hour	Summary of Events and Information	Remarks and references to Appendices
RELY	July 1916 1st		— CORPS RESERVE — Billeted in RELY. Battalion in training. Carried out our few programme ordered. Attack exercises practiced.	
	2nd 3rd 4th		Reinforcements. Other ranks 2 from H.Q. Gly. 7 from L'pool & Garrison Battn. Reb. Battn = 14	
	5th		do. Officers: 1. 2/Lt. R.G. HEPWORTH from 3rd Rif. Fusiliers	
	6th		do. Other ranks 25. from 1st Batt.	
	13th		do. 13.	
			do. Officers: 4. 2/Lt R. WILSON 2/Lt R.E.L. ROBERTS 2/Lt P.L. CLARKE 2/Lt J.M. JONES	
	14th 15th		Battalion moved from FLECHIN Area to CAESTRE by Buses. Battalion carried out training at Billeting area. Battalion moved from CAESTRE to P.1. area by Buses, billeted in Bivouacs.	
	16th 17th 18th 19th		Battalion moved from P.1. area to the line by march route. Relieved 1st R. Dublin Fusiliers in Reserve on CANAL BANK - Left Sector, C/12 (28th November). Relief complete & reported to Brigade about 1.30am (20th Inst.).	
	20th		Battalion employed in making parties & during the day. Relieved 2/R. Lancs. Fusiliers in the Front Line - ZWAANHOF SECTOR. Relief complete & reported at 8.15 am. Got into enemy front line, length 1 officer & 10 O.R. at midnight & by ramp patrols raided 25 yds of front line. Enemy comrades & reservists & NCO advanced 16 tbs of Lance & when they were discovered by a Lt... Rifle & Revolver 26.7.16	

WAR DIARY / INTELLIGENCE SUMMARY

Army Form C. 2118.

(2)

Place	Date	Hour	Summary of Events and Information	Remarks and references to Appendices
	21st		were fired on enemy side. 6 G.S. Bombs were thrown were their heads. Bot located and Patrol on/[taken] from enemy line at 1.30 am. **CASUALTIES** — Nil. **IDENTIFICATIONS** — Nil.	
	21/22		Slight intermittent shelling by the enemy on back areas up to 2am in reply to RED SOS signal shelling Larmi Redan but no difficulty was had in keeping our artillery very active the whole time. Two Aeroplanes sent over at 2 am giving S.O.S. signs and enemy line. One exploded in Trenches rendering 15 minutes Practice Barrage carried out by our artillery commencing at 6 am. Patrols rendered by Covering officers. **CASUALTIES:** Killed 2 O.R. Wounded 11 O.R.	
			Patrol from the Bostic Coy "B" at the Bgt. strength 1 Off + 9 P.R + 1 on Guide at midnight from POST 46. Enemy found to be Working from Gun from C. in CABLE 16. C. in CACTUS with many machine gun fire from Supports. Enemy firing Very Lights freq. Patrol returned at 1.20 am.	
	22		Art Allotment — Trenches shelled from 8.14.11 and C.910 inclusive from 6 am. Intermittent carried out by Artillery. Practice Barrage at 3.30am by our Artillery afterwards by Tanks, Aux Artillery etc. Battalion moved in the withdrawn area (km front line) and Support relieved at 2pm for manoeuvres. 2 Coys (Reserve and Support) relieved at 2pm for manoeuvres. Moved also Reserve to CANAL BANK Wood. In the evening Battalion employed on carrying TM ammunition.	
			An officer's Party of 1 Officer and 6 OR of RGA was approached in front line (C.7.c.o.b) by Sgt Swan (6th Northumb.), who was to be an enemy ship. He was rounded and 6 Capt Bayis Jones. Wounded at 9pm. **CASUALTIES:** wounded 13 OR Killed 12 OR	
	22/23		12 minutes Bombard of L Officer and 8 O.R. sent at end by "B" Coys Joshs. Balt. left and lines at TRENCH. Returned about 1.30 am.	

WAR DIARY
INTELLIGENCE SUMMARY

Army Form C. 2118.

Place	Date	Hour	Summary of Events and Information	Remarks and references to Appendices
	22/23		Enemy sending over Gas Shells and on CRAMP BANK Road on coming back from the Line at about night the air was thick with it in the morning of 23rd.	
	23		Casualties - Gassed 1 officer 7/Lt R.E.W. ROBERTS 24 O.R.	
			Battalion engaged in camping huts during the day mostly T.A. Huniston relieved us in the CANAL BANK West (Left) Bank. Rel. not Bat. Riflno. Moved out in parties of 25, and 3s along track 9+10. DUBLIN CAMP. Relief completed about 2 a.m.	
	23/24		Battalio entry out on Raid on Enemy Trenches at 2 a.m. 24/7/17 known by "B" Coy. Strength 2 officers and 58 other ranks. Commander 2/Lt M.HUGHES JONES. Party arrived at the foot of Boesinghe nearer waiting for the barrage to advance. Enemy were throwing out flares but no fighting was observed. Our officer led his men close to allotted position. Barrage fire opened. Everywhere he penetrated fires and created havoc, he destroyed Gas cylinders out under a 50yd wide enemy trench at eastern plank and more hosed in shell holes may have. The darkness of the night made the work of inspection very hard. Blue rocket were however on enemy batt(?). Enemy sent up 50's of their railway shared with a certainly of fire on 3rd as soon as our fort 30.7.16 a.m. (final). No NANS LAND rifles being used that I knew of the Raid on the [illeg.] on the far side whole(?) and traversed Thompson were made the way hot. No evidence - attempts at unknown Gas Bomb were within a little distance. PLANT/14 R.E.P. at 6.	
			CASUALTIES - (Gassed) 2 O.R. (1 died of wounds (rec.)) N.L.	
	24		Bn. Reme at DUBLIN CAMP. Battalion employed in working parties for "M.A.G."	
			CASUALTIES:- WOUNDED - Gassed 1 Officer 7/Lt W. HUGHES JONES 3 O.R. GASSED 20 O.R.	

WAR DIARY
or
INTELLIGENCE SUMMARY.
(Erase heading not required.)

Army Form C. 2118.

Place	Date	Hour	Summary of Events and Information	Remarks and references to Appendices
	25		Working parties, 50 m. Co. 27 R. supplied by Batt. details (Groups 1) Left Batt. for HERZEELE. CASUALTIES :- 3 O.R. RAISED	
	27		Working parties supplied to H.A.G. also Training Received. Orders from 35th L. STM&D "BY" road 5 none received.	
	28		Battalion Bon details (Groups 1 & 2) relieved 15th R. W. Fusiliers in the front line SWANHOP SECTOR. (Group 2 arrived 18th Brigade Transport Lines' about 10 p.m. REINFORCEMENTS: 30 O.R. CASUALTIES: WOUNDED 3 O.R.	
	29		Battalion in CANAL BANK - Left Sector. Casualties KILLED 1 O.R. WOUNDED 50 O.R.	
	30		Reinforcements 50 O.R. CASUALTIES KILLED 5 WOUNDED 16 O.R. Battalion moved into front line	
	31		At 3.50 a.m. the Batt. in conjunction with 16 details moved in neck monocle attack as part of general scheme of attack on German trenches. Details as per month's diary. CASUALTIES :- 200 O.R. Estimated 7 officers.	

6/8/17

A. M. Molan
Comdg. 16th Bn. L. Cy'L. Pusiloo

WAR DIARY. A.19.a.

16TH BATT. R.W. FUSILIERS.

TO:-
115th Inf. Bde.   Narrative of Operations from 28th July 1917
to 4th August 1917.

Reference, Map, ST JULIEN, 28 N.W. 2, Scale 1/10,000.

28th July -   The Battalion left DUBLIN CAMP on the night of the 28/29th
29th July   July 1917 and proceeded to the ZWAANHOF SECTOR and took
1917.   over from the 15th Batt. R.W. Fusiliers, the line then
             extending from C.7.d.20.25 on the right to C.7.a.20.25 on
             the left - Relief complete at 3.15 a.m. on the 29th July

29th July.   Battalion remained in the front line.
             Casualties, 1 Killed, 1 Wounded and 3 gassed.

30th July.   Battalion still held above mentioned line. Casualties this
             day, 5 Killed, 15 Wounded, and 4 gassed.
             Battalion formed up in their assembly formation, commencing
             at 11p.m., and this was complete at about 2 a.m. on the
             31st July.   Coffee and rum were served out to all men
             previous to ZERO hour.   Trench bridges were placed in
31st July.   position at 2 a.m. on the 31st July.
             The following the position of Companies at ZERO hour:-

             Right front (A) Coy) from C.7.c.25.40. to C.7.c.50.50.

             Left front (B.Coy) were in two waves, first wave from
             C.7.c.5½.7½. to C.7.c.2½.9½ 9½.
             The second wave of this Company was 100 yards in rear and
             parallel to the first.
             A Liaison Patrol was in touch with left flank, and 1st
             Scots Guards on left.

             Right Support (C.Coy) was in position in RAGLAN, HARWICH
             and ESSEX trenches, from C.7.c.1½.7½. to C.7.c.4½.8½.

             Left Support. (D.Coy) was in HARVEY TRENCH from C.7.c.50.50
             to C.7.c.10.50.

             One Section of Vickers Guns, was in ESSEX TRENCH at C.7.c.25.45

             Three Stokes Guns and Teams were in position behind second
             wave of "B" Company.

             Battalion Headquarters were in tunnel dugouts in YORKSHIRE
             TRENCH.

             All wire in front of trenches was cut by parties of the
             Battalion before 1 a.m. on Zero morning.
             Listening posts (2) and a fighting Patrol were kept out
             until 2.50 a.m.

             All Officers and men were at their posts and were in
             readiness for the attack by 3 a.m.

             Punctually at 3.50 a.m. (ZERO hour), the advance commenced
             and as the Barrage came down, men left their assembly
             position and advanced towards the enemy- All lines began to
             move at once, and although the early morning was still dark,
             the lines moved in perfect formation.

July 31st (Contd).

At about 3.55 a.m., the enemy commenced to send over some shells chiefly directed at YORKSHIRE TRENCH and BARNSLEY and all communication trenches.

At 3.57 a.m. the front line of "A" and "B" Companies entered the German front line and advancing with little opposition reached the BLUE LINE at 4.58 a.m.

During this advance, which was most gallantly carried out, opposition was experienced from enemy Machine Guns and Snipers, and several Officers were hit, but the line was in no way retarded or held back. The majority of the enemy met with were dispatched with the bayonet, except those who gave themselves up and were taken prisoners. Rifle fire was little used, and neither were bombs or rifle grenades requisitioned. Lewis Guns came first into play at ZOUAVE HOUSE. About 58 Germans were dispatched during this advance. Hostile opposition was particularly apparent on the left of our advance and casualties were more common in "B" and "D" Companies. Consolidation was begun and carried on well at ZOUAVE HOUSE.

Communication. This was kept up with the 15th Batt.R.W. Fusiliers on the right and with the 1st Scots Guards on the left.

Second Phase.

At 5.5 a.m., "C" and "D" Companies advanced through "A" and "B" and took up the attack on the BLACK LINE, getting up to the barrage just before it lifted at 5.9 a.m. These two Companies, the latter now commanded by their Company Sergeant Major, made excellent progress and overcame the resistance of the hostile groups of the enemy, who were either hidden in block houses or shell holes, and remained until the men either dispatched them or took them prisoners. The numbers of the enemy were now found to be more numerous and seemed to fight with more determination even until they were actually taken by our men. Again little use was made of the bomb, and the rifle and bayonet were largely used. Lewis Guns were only used at periods. Rifle Grenades were not used at all by the men. About 200 of the enemy were accounted for during this advance of my which about 150 were taken prisoners. The opposition of the enemy was more bitter and sustained during the advance from the BLUE to the BLACK LINE. About 3 Machine Guns were captured. The leading Companies reached the BLACK LINE at about 6.5 a.m., and although "D" Company swerved slightly to the right, this was soon rectified, and touch was established with the Guards on the left by a Patrol, sent out by Lieut.J.M.ATTWOOD, and communication was firmly established with the 15th Batt.R.W.Fusiliers on the right. Consolidation was commenced as soon as the BLACK LINE was reached and the position was made secure before 9a.m. By this time all Mopping up was complete behind the BLACK LINE, and only wounded Germans who were quite helpless remained.

At 7.14 a.m., the 15th Batt.R.W.Fusiliers took up the attack on the GREEN LINE, passing though "C" and "D" Coys, and in accordance with instructions "A" and "B" Coys having been relieved by the 13th Batt.R.W.Fusiliers on the BLUE LINE, moved forward and crossed the BLACK LINE at 8a.m. in support to the 15th Batt.R.W.Fusiliers.

The advance of the Battalion to the BLACK LINE had worked perfectly well, and although all the Officers of "D" Company had been put out of action, the Company Sergeant Major carried on at once, and there was no hesitation or delay. A few of the men pushed on dangerously near our own barrage, but no other fault could be found with them. The

31st July (Contd).

and commanded throughout the advance. In many other cases, the Senior surviving Warrant or Non Commissioned Officers carried on at once, and there was no hesitation or dealgy. At times the men pushed on dangerously near our own Barrage, but no other fault could be found with them. The behaviour of all ranks was excellent throughout. The casualties were more severe on the left of the advance, as more resistence was encountered from that direction. Most efficient use was made with the Rifle and Bayonet, and practically little with bombs and grenades, (except in cases of some enemy posts, which held out). All Germans when overtaken or surrounded, surrendered at once or were bayoneted. Lewis Guns were used at times but not to a large extent, but the Rifle was used much more than upon recent operations. Battle outposts were put out at once in front of the BLACK LINE, but these were not called upon to perform any active work. They were also put out on the BLUE LINE but they were only kept out a short time. In this advance the value of Battle outposts did not seem to of as much use since the protective Barrage was quite sufficient to ward off any enemy attack.

The Liaison Patrols kept touch in the first instance, and on the right for the whole of the way; but on the left this Patrol had to hang back, as the 16th Batt.R.W.Fus reached the BLACK LINE before the Guards on the left. Connection was re-established at once on the BLACK LINE. Platoons told off to make good Strong Points in most cases got to their objective, and commenced work at once, but were not joined till some time afterwards by the R.E. ZOUAVE HOUSE and on the BLACK LINE were made good, but little digging was done near TELEGRAPH HOUSE. It is not known when the R.E. joined, but this was some time later.

Runners proved the best means of communication, but the Forward Station was found to be of no use whatever. Battalion Runners need most careful training before an action. It is considered that the Brigade or Battalion Headquarters Signallers should remain in their positions taken up before ZERO hour. More messages would be received and it would be easier to send back messages from forward positions by Runners.

Less Bombs and Rifle Grenades should be carried. The Soldier at present is too heavily loaded for action. Some better protection should be provided in the shape of a cover for Lewis Guns against dust, dirt, or bad weather. The present cover is of little use.

The Carrying parties seemed to work very well indeed. The detachment Machine Gun Company and the Detachment Trench Mortar Battery worked well and got into their respective positions, were not called upon to act. The Battalion Headquarters in three parties, the Second-in Command going up first about 2 hours after ZERO, and the Commanding Officer proceeding later, and the Adjutant, when Battalion Headquarters was established at TELEGRAPH HOUSE. It is considered best, that, if Battalion Headquarters has to move, one move should only be made, and that to a definite place where it should be established and should remain there.

31st July.

Third Phase.

"A" and "B" Companies after advancing over the BLACK LINE remained in reserve to the 15th R.W.Fusiliers and were in position under 2nd/Lieut W.J.WILLIAMS just behind IRON CROSS - (U.26.d.9.8), until the Battalion was withdrawn

31st July (Contd).	by the order of the Brigadier General Commanding, to HARVEY TRENCH. "C" and "D" Companies remained in their position on the BLACK LINE till about 6 p.m. when they were withdrawn to HARVEY TRENCH. "A" and "B" Companies were withdrawn from the above position at about midnight on the night of 31st July/1st August, and rejoined the Battalion in HARVEY TRENCH.
1st August.	The Battalion returned to the front line at 7 p.m. on 1st Aug 1917, and relieved the 15th Welsh in Posts just in front of STRAY FARM, relief complete at 3.30 a.m. on the 2nd August. The Battalion Headquarters being at STRAY FARM and the Battalion was now in support of 2 Companies of the 10th South Wales Borderers, who were in front on the banks of the STEENBECK.
2nd August.	The 113th Inf. Brigade took over the whole of the front line, the 15th Batt. R.W. Fusiliers relieving the 10th S.W.B. in front and the 16th Batt. R.W. Fusiliers remained in Support.
3rd August.	On the 3rd August, one line of Posts was withdrawn about 300 yards as the enemy shelling became very severe and many casualties resulted. The Battalion remained in this position
4th August.	until 6 p.m on the evening of the 4th August, when it was relieved by the 15th Welsh Regiment, the relief being complete at 7.15 p.m. on that date.
5th August	Battalion marched to ELVERDINGHE CHATEAU, and afterwards entrained on the 5th August for PROVEN AREA.

The weather throughout was deplorable and during nearly the whole of the above period the men were up to their knees in mud and water and the hardships on all ranks were great, but were most cheerfully borne.

The spirit of all ranks was excellent and the dash of the Battalion in the attack on the 31st July was beyond all expectation. The losses were unusually severe, but could not have been avoided, as even the advent of the rain made the ground so soft and muddy that many casualties were thereby saved.

Lieut Col.,
Commanding, 16th Batt. R.W. Fusrs.

In the Field.
7th Aug. 1917.

Vol 21

16th Battn. Royal Welsh Fusiliers

War Diary

August - 1917

21 F
10 mark

WAR DIARY or INTELLIGENCE SUMMARY

Army Form C. 2118.

16th Bn Royal Welch Fus
113th Infantry Bde.
38th (Welsh) Division

Place: August

Date	Hour	Summary of Events and Information	Remarks and references to Appendices
Aug 1st		The Battalion was relieved and dugouts about FLASH POINT after carrying out attack on previous day, as per narrative attached.	
	1pm	Battalion returned to front line, relieving the 15th Welch in front, just in front of STRAY FARM, relief complete at 3.30 a.m. on the 2nd Aug.	
2nd		The Battalion remained in support, the 15th Bn RWF relieving the 10th SWB in the front line.	
3rd		Owing to severe enemy shelling one line of posts was withdrawn about 30 yards. This line was held until the Bn was relieved by the 15th Welch Regt at 6pm on the evening of the 4th Aug, the relief being complete by 7.15 pm. The Bn proceeded in small parties to ELVERDINGHE CHATEAU where the men were provided with a hot meal, clean changes of underclothing and khaki. The Divisional Canteen provided cigarettes, matches, chocolate and biscuits. The night was spent in the CHATEAU. A Narrative of the action is attached.	

Casualties from 31st July to 4th Aug inclusive

Officers   1 Died of Wounds.   9 Wounded
Other Ranks   9 Died of Wounds   182 Wounded   33 Killed
     13 O.R. Missing

WAR DIARY
or
INTELLIGENCE SUMMARY.

Army Form C. 2118.

Place	Date	Hour	Summary of Events and Information	Remarks and references to Appendices
	Aug 4		Reinforcements:- Other Ranks 26. Rewards for service in the field:- Distinguished Service Order. Major S.L. Hinkins. Military Cross. Capt. H. Payne Lieut. J.M. Attwell 2/Lt. W.J. Cott 2/Lt. W.J. Williams Distinguished Conduct Medal 18261 C.S.M. Roberts J.A 12458 Sgt L.C. Roberts 19428 Cpl. Geo. J. English Bar to D.C.M. 18539 Sgt. W. Jones Military Medal. 20144 Sgt. J. Foley 18034 Pte. H.J. Jones 19377 L/Cpl. T. Jenkins 19232 Pte. G.J. Griffiths 18569 Sgt. J. Gray 18946 Pte. R. Prichard 18537 Sgt. H. Davies 24771 L/Cpl. H. Pearce 55812 Sgt. E. Scott 50857 Pte. H. Pye 19736 L/Cpl. W.S. Davies Bar to Military Medal 24768 Cpl. H.J. McGuinn	

Army Form C. 2118.

WAR DIARY
or
INTELLIGENCE SUMMARY.
(Erase heading not required.)

Instructions regarding War Diaries and Intelligence Summaries are contained in F. S. Regs., Part II. and the Staff Manual respectively. Title pages will be prepared in manuscript.

Place	Date	Hour	Summary of Events and Information	Remarks and references to Appendices
	Aug 5th		The Battalion entrained at ELVERDINGHE and proceeded to PROVEN, and thence by march route to FIELDS at PERSIA CAMP. Remainder of the day spent in rest.	
	6th		Cleaning equipment etc. Inspection of kit and replacement of deficiencies. Party of 12 Other Ranks, reported at ELVERDINGHE CHATEAU, to be employed as burial party.	
	7th to 17th		Training carried out at PERSIA CAMP as per programme issued. Full use made of Baths at GOUTHOVE. Firing on range at HERZEELE 16th and 17th Aug.	
			Reinforcements:—	
			11th Aug 1 Officer 1 Other Ranks 2/Lt. E.M. Madoc Jones	
			15th " 1 " 1 " 2/Lt. V. P. Williams	
			18 " 1 "	
			18 " 153 Other Ranks	
	18th		In accordance with orders the Battalion left PERSIA CAMP at 5.30 hrs and proceeded by march route to PROVEN. Entrained and proceeded to ELVERDINGHE. Halted for the night at GARDOEN FARM. Details sent to CORPS REINFORCEMENT CAMP at HERZEELE and details to H. Camp.	

Army Form C. 2118.

WAR DIARY
or
INTELLIGENCE SUMMARY.
(Erase heading not required.)

Place	Date	Hour	Summary of Events and Information	Remarks and references to Appendices
	Aug. 19	3.30	Battalion proceeded by march route from CARDEN FARM to bivouacs at C.22.d.7.8. in the MALAKOFF FARM area. Field kitchens moved off prior to Bn. and had tea ready on arrival at bivouac.	
	20		Training carried out as per programme. Enemy aircraft very active, especially about 10 p.m. when a number of bombs were dropped. Assisted by air searchlights the Anti Aircraft Guns and machine guns opened a fairly heavy fire when the aeroplane became visible.	
	21		Carried on with training. Enemy aircraft very active during the afternoon. Bombs were dropped nr/ also nr/ the camp. More bombs were dropped after dark.	
	22	7pm	Proceeded to W. CANAL BANK and relieved the 16th Welch Regt. Billeted on CANAL BANK, and dugouts on the ZWAANHOF sector. Supplied working party of 350 O.R. for cable burying. Off-loading and filling in shell holes. CASUALTIES 1 O.R. Wounded (att. Lewing Co.)	
	23/28.		Supplied carrying parties, off-loading, and cable burying parties. Training under Company arrangements also carried out. Training 24 Aug. 1 O.R. at R.E. Wounded 27 " " 2/3 Wounded	

WAR DIARY
INTELLIGENCE SUMMARY

Place	Date	Hour	Summary of Events and Information	Remarks and references to Appendices
	Aug 30		Battalion relieved the 11th Bn S.W.B in the front line, relief commenced 10 pm and completed about 1 am. C & D Companies in the front line A Coy in support and B Coy in reserve. Battalion Headquarters at ALOUETTE FARM. Details to H Camp and Transport Lines. CASUALTIES 9 OR wounded (1 since died of wounds)	
	31		The Battalion held the line as above.	

M. Carter
Capt & Adjutant

A. Lush Col. MW Jardine C.M.G
Commdt. 16th Batt. R.W.F.

1.9.17

16th Batt. Royal Welsh Fusiliers.

Vol 22

War Diary

for

September 1917.

WAR DIARY
or
INTELLIGENCE SUMMARY.

Army Form C. 2118.

16th Bn Royal Welch Fus.
113th Infantry Brigade
38th (Welsh) Division

September

Place	Date	Hour	Summary of Events and Information	Remarks and references to Appendices
	Sept 1st		Batts. holding Nights Bn Sector, LANGEMARCK Sector. Disposition as follows — 2 Companies in the front line and 2 Companies in Support. Battalion Headquarters at ALOUETTE FARM. In the evening relieved by the 13th Battn Royal Welch Fusiliers, relief complete about 11 p.m. Battalion moved to Support Line, Battn Headquarters being at AU BON GITE. ALOUETTE FARM heavily shelled throughout the day, chiefly with H.V. guns. CASUALTIES. O.Ranks. KILLED 5 WOUNDED 10. MISSING 2.	
	2.		Holding Support Line as taken over on previous day. Enemy aircraft very active, flying very low and firing on the men with machine guns. AU BON GITE received a good deal of attention from enemy artillery. CASUALTIES. O.Ranks WOUNDED 1.	
	3/4.		Holding line as above. Enemy aeroplanes again very active, and in addition to engaging our men with machine guns, dropped a pamphlet which was picked up by a runner and taken to Bn Headquarters. On the night of the 4/5th the Battalion was relieved by the 14th Bn Welsh Regt. In accordance with March Table the Battalion moved	

WAR DIARY or INTELLIGENCE SUMMARY

Army Form C. 2118.

Place	Date	Hour	Summary of Events and Information	Remarks and references to Appendices
	2.9.18 4/5th		to the MALAKOFF AREA (B 22 d.5.7.) Taking over tramways etc from the 17th Bn Royal Welsh Fusiliers. CASUALTIES O.Ranks WOUNDED 5	
	5th		The day devoted to cleaning up and checking efficiency in equipment etc. Camp inspection by the Commanding Officer and Company Commanders for inspection in the afternoon.	
	6th 7th 8th 9th		Carried out training in the above area as per programmes and supplied working parties as called for. Enemy aircraft very active after nightfall, a number of bombs were dropped. On the night of the 8/9th the camp was shelled with about eight shells of about 8" calibre. REINFORCEMENTS O.Ranks = 52.	
	6th Sept			
	10th		The morning was spent in cleaning up the camp and packing stores etc. Battalion paraded in full marching order at 1.15 pm. Proceeded by march route to ELVERDINGHE, entrained to INTERNATIONAL CORNER and thence by march route to S2 Area, SWINDON CAMP.	
	11/12		Training carried out as per programmes. See rear of the forthcoming	

WAR DIARY
or
INTELLIGENCE SUMMARY.
(Erase heading not required.)

Army Form C. 2118.

Place	Date	Hour	Summary of Events and Information	Remarks and references to Appendices
	11/13		march, a route march was included in each day's training.	
			REINFORCEMENTS. 11/9/17. OFFICERS:- 2/Lt E Thomas 2/Lt H R Evans " W O Evans " H Bennett. " L Hughes. " D H Harries 13/9/17. 2/Lt J R Warren.	
	14th		In accordance with the Divisional move, the Battn marched to EECKE, passing starting point (X.28.c.9.0.) at 10.27a.m. The field kitchens cooked dinner on kind of march. Halt from 1.30 until 3.45. Arrived at EECKE about 6 p.m.	
	15th		Advance party preceded by two to the new area, and were attached to the 172nd Infantry Brigade until the time was taken over by the Battn. Battalion marched to the MORBECQUE area in accordance with march table, arriving billets 1.30 p.m.	
	16th		Starting 9 a.m. the Battn proceeded by march route to the SAILLY-SUR-LA-LYS area. Dinner served on route of march. Arrived billets 6.15 p.m.	
	17th		In accordance with Brigade Order, the 16th Bn R.W.F relieved the 2/4 Bn South Lancashire Regt, as B/L Battalion in the BOIS GRENIER Section. DISPOSITION:- B, C and D Companies in Support Line A Company in Subsidiary Line. A fifth Company (from 13th Bn R.W.Fus.) was attached, and accommodated in Unterlands V/5795. CASUALTIES. O.Ranks: 1 wounded.	

WAR DIARY
or
INTELLIGENCE SUMMARY.
(Erase heading not required.)

Army Form C. 2118.

Place	Date	Hour	Summary of Events and Information	Remarks and references to Appendices
	18		Day quiet. Aircraft fairly active, both enemy and our own. Patrol went out at midnight 18/19 at Cross Roads I.16.a.66.05, and proceeded along road leading S.E. Strength of patrol 1 Officer, 11 O.R. No enemy encountered. Returned at 2.18 a.m. at same point as out. REINFORCEMENTS:— OFFICERS:— 2/Lt J.J.Linton	
	19	9.30–10.30	Intermittent firing by 18 pdr. On enemy wire and front line. This was repeated between 7 p.m. and 8 p.m.	
		7.35 & 8.25	Heavy Trench Mortars on our front line I.16.1 to I.16/3 and on Leith Walk and Nur Jan at I.16.a.8.2. H.E. Shrapnel over Lille Post and Orchard Line, and heavy T.Ms. on Buz, also Biez. Heavy T.Ms on front at I.20.a.67. Our Light T.Ms fired in retaliation to above fire. During the bombardment enemy sent up signal lights along whole front from I.12/1 to I.16/3, twenty into 6 rows. Enemy plane flying low over our lines also dropped 3 flaming white lights. No result observed. At dawn 2 Russian journeys of war crossed no mans land and entered our trenches at I.2.5. having escaped from the enemy during the night. CASUALTIES OFFICERS:— 2/Lt W.J.Williams Killed. OTHER RANKS:— KILLED — 11. WOUNDED 21. (4 DIED OF WOUNDS.)	
	20		Very little activity during the day. Enemy aeroplanes crossed lines during the day and were engaged by our A.A guns and machine guns. One plane came down escaping from our aeroplanes & fired a lewis gun from active. Two escaped German prisoners reported escaped from the support trenches WEST MESSINES at about midnight. They had escaped from the	

Army Form C. 2118.

WAR DIARY
or
INTELLIGENCE SUMMARY.
(Erase heading not required.)

Place	Date	Hour	Summary of Events and Information	Remarks and references to Appendices
	20		18th S.L.W Camp Mar. STONER. Several bursts of hostile Machine Gun fire during the night, directed chiefly against back areas. Patrol reported to examine wire and movements in No Man's Land. CASUALTIES — O.Ranks 3 slightly (at duty) 3 wd. (add wds)	
	21	9 a.m.	Very little artillery activity during the day. 2 Planes (unknown breed) brought down enemy lines near WEZ MACQUART.	
		12.25 p.m.	Two enemy planes chased our 2 artillery scouts out Cairo I 21/4 at about 200 feet. Hostile machine gunners engaged by Lewis machine fire, and our machines occupied. Intermittent machine gun fire during the night. REINFORCEMENTS. O.RANKS 17.	
	22		A little intermittent artillery fire during the day. Enemy aircraft very active at dusk. Patrolled this lines inside in surprise on Centre Bn. through the lines found at 9 p.m. Enemy I 21/5. Patrol was moving EAST and was fired on by Lewis at I 21 or 90.80. and showing particularly sent out our artillery fire destroyed. Fighting patrols out 1 own men and 1 English returned. Misty - throwing out flares during the morning, and there was a fair amount of aerial activity. The Battalion was relieved by the 13th Battn. R.W.Fus. on the nights 23/24. Marched back to billets at ERQUINGHEM, leaving "A" as a fifth Coy attached to 13th Battn. R.W.F. on Subsidiary Line. CASUALTIES OTHER RANKS — 2 WOUNDED.	
	23			
	24		The day devoted to cleaning up. Supplied Sh Ling fatigues, and a carrying party, as per ERQUINGHEM trench diary orders.	

Army Form C. 2118.

WAR DIARY
or
INTELLIGENCE SUMMARY.
(Erase heading not required.)

Instructions regarding War Diaries and Intelligence Summaries are contained in F.S. Regs., Part II and the Staff Manual respectively. Title pages will be prepared in manuscript.

Place	Date	Hour	Summary of Events and Information	Remarks and references to Appendices
	25 May		Carried out training and supplied fatigue parties as on previous day.	
	26		Carried out training during the morning. Had Battalion Sports in Bristol Field in the afternoon. "B" Coy relieved "A" Coy as fifth Coy attached to the 13th Bn R.W.F. "C" Coy left the trenches but coy att 13th Bn R.W.F. Supplied fatigue parties as before.	
	27th 28th		Training and fatigue parties as on previous days. Battalion concert in the Cinema on the night of the 29th. Divisional Band in attendance. 2/Lt REINFORCEMENTS. OFFICERS:- 2/Lt T.B. PRICE " WYOUNG.	
	29.		Training and fatigues as on previous days. The Battalion relieved the 13th Bn R.W.F. as Left Battalion BOIS GRENIER Sector. "C" Coy from the Subsidiary Line relieved the Centre Coy 13th Regt. "B" Remained in the Subsidiary Line as support Coy. "A" and "D" Coys (from ERQUINGHEM) relieved the Right and Left Companies of the 13th Bn R.W.F. respectively. Relief reported complete 10.45 p.m. Fighting patrols left our line I.21.c.45.90 at 4.30 am. 20# 40 ### in road near I.21.c.60.50, and patrolled military training and fighting lines Enemy machine guns firing busy on road. Hostile planes flying low and over our outposts during the night.	

2353 Wt. W2544/1454 700,000 5/15 D.D.& L. A.D.S.S./Form/C.2118.

WAR DIARY
or
INTELLIGENCE SUMMARY.

(Erase heading not required.)

Army Form C. 2118.

Place	Date	Hour	Summary of Events and Information	Remarks and references to Appendices
	Sept 29		quiet from dusk to 10 p.m.	
	30		Artillery quiet. Hostile aeroplanes very active, and were heavily engaged by our A.A. Guns, Machine Guns & Lewis Guns. Enemy O.P. appeared to be considerably nearer the line than usual. Our aircraft nothing active.	
			CASUALTIES. OTHER RANKS. 1 WOUNDED	

J.M. Jourdain Lieut Col.
Commanding, 14th Bn Royal Welch Fus.

16th BATT ROYAL WELSH FUSILIERS. Vol 23

WAR DIARY
FOR
OCTOBER 1917.

23 F
10 shuts

WAR DIARY or INTELLIGENCE SUMMARY.

Army Form C. 2118.

16th Bn Royal Welch Fus
113th Infantry Bde
38th (Welsh) Division

Place	Date	Hour	Summary of Events and Information	Remarks and references to Appendices
	Oct. 1917 1st		Battalion holding the LEFT SECTION BOIS GRENIER. Very little artillery activity during the day. At 11 a.m. the enemy attempted to "line up" on BURNT FARM. Aerial activity below normal. Two trench & mortars & machine gun fire on the ROAD behind SUBSIDIARY LINE from dusk onwards. Our Lewis guns fired on spots during the night.	
		2.45 pm	Small red balloon sent from enemy line and crossed our line at WILLOW AVENUE. A Fighting patrol of 1 Officer + 10 O.R. sent out line at I.21.a.75.20 at 9 p.m. but no enemy patrols were engaged. Reconnaissance patrols examined our own and the enemy wire.	
	2nd	10.30 pm	Intermittent shelling in front of SUBSIDIARY LINE with 4.2 hour. Desultory shelling of our support line at 11 a.m. with 77 mm. Enemy aerial activity very slight except from dusk to midnight. At 10.45 hostile plane fired into LEFT FRONT Coy trenches, and was engaged by our AA and machine gun fire. Patrol reports that enemy trench running S.E. from pond at I.15.d.4.1. to a recessed sap about 70' long, ending in 2 post dugouts in front of the old mine. Fighting patrol also turned out, but two enemy patrols were met.	
	3rd		Owing to that morally there was very little aerial or artillery activity during the day, with the exception of a rapid burst of 12 rds 77 mm.	

Army Form C. 2118.

WAR DIARY
or
INTELLIGENCE SUMMARY.
(Erase heading not required.)

Place	Date	Hour	Summary of Events and Information	Remarks and references to Appendices
	3rd.	12-1 pm	Behind the ORCHARD about I.15.c. and again about 12.30pm Enemy sniper about I.21.d. 40.85 fired 13 shots at periscope at AUDREY POST I.21.a.70.10. and obtained 2 hits. Our 18 pdrs fired 20 rds on INCLEMENT TRENCH and SUPPORT LINE in retaliation for 77mm on ORCHARD. Reconnaissance patrols went out to examine enemy wire and condition of disused trenches E. and S.E. of CHARD FARM. A fighting patrol went out but didn't encounter any enemy patrols.	
	4th.		Practically no artillery activity. Hostile machine guns fired on RAILWAY and ROAD behind SUBSIDIARY LINE during the night. Our Lewis Guns fired on gaps from 10.30pm. to midnight. Three reconnaissance patrols went out to examine enemy wire and ditches in front of trenches. Fighting patrol went out but no enemy encountered. Several rockets bursting into double red sent up opposite Left Coy front. Only rockets observed were 2 IMB firing into our line about I.16.a. 79.02. REINFORCEMENTS: OFFICERS: 2/Lt W. OWEN 2/Lt J.L. RALPH 2/Lt D.E. LEWIS 2/Lt T.S. WILLIAMS.	
	5th.	2.20pm 5 pm 2.45- 6.5pm	Enemy aircraft fairly busy over our lines, especially about 5.45 pm and 6.15 pm Our artillery carried out destruction shoot on INCLEMENT TRENCH. Wire cutting I.26.b. 77.30. REINFORCEMENTS: OFFICERS: 2/Lt B. DAVIES	

Army Form C. 2118.

WAR DIARY
or
INTELLIGENCE SUMMARY.
(Erase heading not required.)

Instructions regarding War Diaries and Intelligence Summaries are contained in F.S. Regs., Part II. and the Staff Manual respectively. Title pages will be prepared in manuscript.

Place	Date	Hour	Summary of Events and Information	Remarks and references to Appendices
	5th		The Battalion was relieved in the LEFT SECTION BOIS GRENIER by the 13th Battn. Royal Welch Fusiliers. Two Companies 16th Bn R.W.F. remained in SUBSIDIARY LINE attached to 13th Bn R.W.F. The two other Companies returned to billets in ERQUINGHEM. Relief complete 11 p.m. REINFORCEMENTS. OFFICERS: 2/Lt TEVANS.	
	6th		Day devoted to cleaning up and inspection by Company Commanders. Supplied fatigue parties as per ERQUINGHEM Standing Orders.	
	7th		No training carried out. As 1 coy. all nights find fatigue from midnight til reveille tout.	
	8th		Training carried out as per programme. In the evening 2 Companies from billets relieved 2 Companies in SUBSIDIARY LINE. The Coys from SUBS. LINE returning to billets in ERQUINGHEM. REINFORCEMENTS: OTHER RANKS: 7 CASUALTIES: OTHER RANKS 1 KILLED 4 WOUNDED (of 2nd Lt) DIED OF WDS	
	9th 10th		Training carried out as per programme. Supplied fatigue parties as per ERQUINGHEM Standing orders.	
	11th		Carried out training during the day. In the evening the 16th Bn R.W.F. relieved the 13th Bn RWF in LEFT Sector BOIS GRENIER. Relief complete 11.30 p.m. B Co. from SUBS LINE relieved CENTRE FRONT 13th R.W.F. C " " " " SUPPORT " D " " " " RIGHT FRONT 13th R.W.F. A " BILLETS " LEFT "	

Army Form C. 2118.

WAR DIARY
or
INTELLIGENCE SUMMARY.

(Erase heading not required.)

Instructions regarding War Diaries and Intelligence Summaries are contained in F. S. Regs., Part II. and the Staff Manual respectively. Title pages will be prepared in manuscript.

4.

Place	Date	Hour	Summary of Events and Information	Remarks and references to Appendices
	11th		Attached troops of the 19th Bn CEF were taken over from the 13th Bn RWR and the remainder of the wire run.	
	12th		Recently normal. 2 p.m. to 4.30 p.m. one Flight carried out wire cutting about I.21.c.25.02. Our 2" DMs fired 98 rounds on INCLINE SUPPORT I.27.a.00.45 to I.27.a.30.75. Enemy trench and wire (2076 "Flint") Enemy mounting gun very active against our aircraft.	
		12.30 p.m.	3 hostile planes unsuccessfully attacked one of our observation planes. Patrols sent out to examine wire etc. No enemy patrol engaged.	
	13th		Very little activity during the day. Enemy machine gun fire heavy on the ROAD behind SUBSIDIARY LINE I.14.d.40.80. Aircraft inactive owing to bad visibility. Our officers and 6 O.R. off our line at I.16.c.6.8 to reconnoitre gaps in enemy wire and locate enemy posts. Posts located at I.22.a.60.82. Wire found to be strong and continuous at this point. No gaps were discovered 13th Bn R.W.R. also sent out 2 patrols from the CENTRE COY FRONT.	
	14th	3 p.m. –5.15 p.m.	2" DMs fired on enemy line at I.21.c.50.15, and trench at I.27.a.50.85. Damage done to trench and wire.	
		3 p.m.	Stokes guns opened deliberate fire on INCLINE SUPPORT and fired 212 rnds.	
		2.10 p.m.	Enemy fired 30 nds 10.5 cm. shells round DEAD COW FARM I.20.d. and WILLOW AV. I.20.d. in retaliation to our 2 M.G. bombardment.	
		3.50 p.m.	Hostile DMs retaliated their shoot on I.21.c.00.75 and support lines.	

Army Form C. 2118.

WAR DIARY
or
INTELLIGENCE SUMMARY.
(Erase heading not required.)

Instructions regarding War Diaries and Intelligence Summaries are contained in F. S. Regs., Part II. and the Staff Manual respectively. Title pages will be prepared in manuscript.

Place	Date	Hour	Summary of Events and Information	Remarks and references to Appendices
	14th		Enemy machine gun fire along SUBS. LINE during night. Our Lewis guns fired upon the gaps during the night. Hostile aircraft very active during the afternoon, 12 planes being up at one time. Fighting patrol and reconnaissance patrols sent out during the night, but no enemy patrols encountered.	
	15th		Activity normal during whole day. At 9pm a variety of coloured lights reported behind enemy line (probably as guides to aircraft) Lewis guns fired on gaps during the night. Fighting patrol of 1 Officer and 10 OR left our line at 1.15.d.30.10. at 6.6 pm to verify location of enemy post at I.22.a.60.75. Enemy wiring party of about 40 OR plainly seen hotly encountering to fill up gaps, these then settled along the day directly in front of post I.22.a.60.75, moving very slow to pamphlet. No action taken owing to the own numerical superiority of the enemy.	
	16th		Aircraft machine. Our medium TM's fired on INCLINE TRENCH between 3.15 pm and 4.30 pm. Stokes guns retaliated to hostile TM's on INCLINE SUPPORT 30 rounds fired. Patrol of 1 Officer and 25 ORs and 2 signallers left our line at I.35.d.35.10 at 6 p.m. with the object of taking action against enemy working party at I.22.a.60.75. and use all means to obtain identification. Patrol worked until 8.30 pm. But no enemy working party was seen. Patrol then returned according to programme. CASUALTIES. OTHER RANKS. 2 WOUNDED (1 accidental)	

Army Form C. 2118.

WAR DIARY
or
INTELLIGENCE SUMMARY.

(Erase heading not required.)

Instructions regarding War Diaries and Intelligence Summaries are contained in F. S. Regs., Part II. and the Staff Manual respectively. Title pages will be prepared in manuscript.

Place	Date	Hour	Summary of Events and Information	Remarks and references to Appendices
	17th		Enemy artillery quiet on forward area, but slight shelling round WELLINGTON AVE. and I.14.d. 40.80. Three enemy planes patrolled back areas all day. Our aircraft active during the afternoon and evening. Patrol of 1 Officer and 10 O.R. left our line at I.15. & 30.05. at 7.30 p.m. to lie in wait for any enemy attempting to repair wire opposite I.22.a.60.78. No enemy party encountered. Enemy found at this point to be very small. 16th Bn R.W.F. relieved by the 13th Bn R.W.F., 2 Companies 16th Bn R.W.F. remained in the SUBS. LINE, attached 13th Bn R.W.F. The other two Coys returned to billets in ERQUINGHEM. Relief complete 8.30 p.m.	
	18th		Day devoted to cleaning up and checking of stores and equipment. Patrol & fatigue parties as per standing orders.	
	19/20		Training carried out as per programme, also provided fatigue parties as above. During evening the 20th the two Coys from ERQUINGHEM relieved the two Coys in SUBS. LINE, the 2 Coys from SUBS. LINE returning to billets in ERQUINGHEM.	
	21st		No training carried out. The 2 Coys from the line spent the day in cleaning up etc. Fatigue parties supplied as above. REINFORCEMENTS:- OFFICERS: 2/Lt W.A. BRODIE OTHER RANKS 8.	
	22/23		Training carried out as per programme. Fatigue parties supplied as above. On the evening of the 23rd the 16th Bn R.W.F. relieved the 13th Bn R.W.F. in the LEFT SECTOR BOIS GRENIER. Relief complete 2 Coys 10th Bn C.E.P. 8.10 p.m.	

WAR DIARY
or
INTELLIGENCE SUMMARY.
(Erase heading not required.)

Army Form C. 2118.

Place	Date	Hour	Summary of Events and Information	Remarks and references to Appendices
	23		were taken over from the 13th Bn KRRC, and were attached for instructions. Patrol sent out to reconnoitre supposed gap in enemy wire at farm I.16.c.65.00. No gap found at this front. Our other patrols also left our line but no enemy patrols were encountered.	
	24	10.50 am 11.40 am	Our artillery carried out wire cutting I.16.d.55.98./I.16.d.70.05. Destructive shots on INCLEMENT SUPPORT. 3 pm to 4.15 pm our 6" Stokes guns	
		12.15 pm	fired 30 rds on WEZ MACQUART. 3 pm Stokes guns fired on INCLEMENT TRENCH, SUPPORT and SWITCH as a diversion for 6" 2MB. 110 rds fired. Retaliation on INDEX SUPPORT and INCREASE SUPPORT 70 rds fired	
		7.30 am 8.30 am	Few 77 mm shells on front line (CHARD FARM) MINE AV. and again at 12.30 pm when 8 77 mm Few 10.5 cm shells on MINE AV. and again at 12.30 pm when 8 77 mm rounds fired. Enemy aircraft normally active. 2 reconnoitring patrols went out to inspect our wire and to verify suspected listening post at I.21.d.3.5. Owing to darkness and rain "going" was very difficult, no enemy encountered.	
	25		Activity rather normal. 3 hostile aeroplanes crossed our lines at 11 km. until two aeroplanes enemy aircraft were inactive. 2 reconnaissance patrols and 1 fighting patrol left our lines, but no hostile patrols were met. Enemy working party heard driving in stakes and talking at I.21.c.50.28. by end of the reconnaissance patrol. Nos 3 and 4 Coys relieved Nos 1 and 2 Coys C.E.P. under own arrangements.	
			CASUALTIES. OTHER RANKS 1 Accidentally Wounded.	

WAR DIARY or INTELLIGENCE SUMMARY

Army Form C. 2118.

Place	Date	Hour	Summary of Events and Information	Remarks and references to Appendices
	26th	11.30 a.m.	Enemy fired about 20 rds 77mm on EILEEN POST and about 20 rds on WINE and COWGATE C.Ts. otherwise artillery quiet. Between 3 p.m. & 4.20 p.m. 2" T.Ms. fired 80 rds on INCLEMENT SUPPORT and our 3" Stokes guns fired 110 rds on INCLINE and INCLUDE SUPPORTS, silencing enemy T.M. activity during the morning. Enemy aircraft active. Three patrols sent out till 1 a.m. no enemy engaged.	
	27th		Little artillery activity except in rear areas. Aerial activity above normal. Three hostile planes at about 1000 ft over rear areas, apparently regulating for heavy artillery shoot on ARMENTIERS - 9.20 a.m. - 10.20 a.m. Our ack-ack did nothing. Patrol of 1 Officer and 16 O.R. (British) and 9 O.R. (Portuguese) left our line 10 p.m. I 21. a. 90. 05. to locate enemy running parties suspected at gap I 21. d. 05. 85. Returned about 12.15 a.m. but no enemy party seen. 2 reconnaissance patrols also went out.	
	28		REINFORCEMENTS: OTHER RANKS: 15. Intermittent shelling of WINE, COWGATE, and WELLINGTON C.Ts. with 77 mm. Aerial activity above normal. One of our riflemen drove enemy reconnaissance machine back over his own line at 11.10 a.m. At dusk the attached Nos 3 & 4 Coys 10th Bn. C.E.P. moved out of the line & relieved	
		9.30 p.m.	Special by R.E.s projected 1183 gas bombs from Batty front. Enemy gas	
		9.45 p.m.	alarms were sounded opposite right leg front about 2 minutes after the	

Army Form C. 2118.

WAR DIARY
or
INTELLIGENCE SUMMARY.
(Erase heading not required.)

Instructions regarding War Diaries and Intelligence Summaries are contained in F. S. Regs., Part II. and the Staff Manual respectively. Title pages will be prepared in manuscript.

Place	Date	Hour	Summary of Events and Information	Remarks and references to Appendices
	28.		Opening of bombardment. Alarm spread quietly and a rocket bursting into 5 gold stars was sent up from INCLINE SUPPORT towards rear and a green Very light towards ANNIE'S POST. The enemy appeared to expect a raid and set up many Very lights. Alarm bells could be heard ringing in the rear and the line. After the shelling ceased, ie, about 11.15 p.m. Concentration the enemy fired on ORCHARD and close SUPPORT LINE with H.E. many of which were "duds".	
	29.	5.30 a.m.	Enemy raiding party entered our trenches on the left of CYNTHIA POST and were engaged by the garrison of this trench. Two wounded prisoners remained in our hands. Our casualties were two OR slightly wounded. During the morning the Bn. was relieved by the 13th Bn R.S. Fus. Two Coys 16th Bn R.S. remained on SUBS LINE, the other two Coys returned to billets at ERAVINGHEM. CASUALTIES: OTHER RANKS: 1 KILLED, 7 WOUNDED	
	30th 31st		Carried out training as per programme. On morning of 31st the Brigadier General Commanding inspected the billets of 2 Coys in Reserve and presented parchment certificates to men of B + C Coys.	

R.W. Mondair Lieut. Col.
Commanding 16th Bn R.W. Fusiliers

16th BATT. ROYAL WELSH FUSILIERS

WAR DIARY

FOR

NOVEMBER 1917

WAR DIARY
or
INTELLIGENCE SUMMARY.

Army Form C. 2118.

16th Bn Royal Welsh Fusiliers
113th Infantry Brigade,
38th (Welsh) Division.

November 1917

Place	Date	Hour	Summary of Events and Information	Remarks and references to Appendices
	Nov. 1917 1st		Battalion Headquarters and 2 Companies in billets in ERQUINGHEM, and 2 Companies in the SUBSIDIARY LINE, LEFT SUB-SECTOR BOIS GRENIER, attached to the 13th Bn R.W.Fus. Supplied fatigue parties as called for in ERQUINGHEM standing Orders, and carried out training as per programme. During the evening the 2 Companies from billets in ERQUINGHEM (B&C) relieved the 2 Companies (D&A) in the SUBSIDIARY LINE.	
	2nd		Supplied fatigue parties as above, and carried out training as per programme.	
	3rd		Supplied fatigue parties as above, and carried out training as per programme. 'B' Coy 16th Bn R.W.F. were relieved in RIGHT RESE by No 4 Coy 10th Bn C.E.P. 'C' " " " " " LEFT RESE " "A" Coy 13th Bn R.W.F. 'B' & 'C' Companies 16th Bn R.W.Fus. returning to billets in ERQUINGHEM.	
	4th		Carried out training as per programme, and supplied fatigue parties in accordance with Standing Orders. In the evening the 16th Bn R.W.F. relieved the 13th Bn R.W.F. in the LEFT SUB-SECTOR BOISGRENIER as under:- 'A' Coy 16th Bn R.W.Fus relieved 'C' Coy 13th R.W.F. in LEFT FRONT 'D' " " " " " " " " RESERVE.	

WAR DIARY
or
INTELLIGENCE SUMMARY.
(Erase heading not required.)

Army Form C. 2118.

Place	Date	Hour	Summary of Events and Information	Remarks and references to Appendices
	Nov.1917.			
	4th	8.30 p.m.	Relief complete 8.30 p.m. Right half Batt'n front being held by the 10th Bn C.E.P.	
			REINFORCEMENTS - 2 O.Rs.	
	5th		In view of the enterprise to be carried out shortly, 'C' Coy (in BILLETS in ERQUINGHEM) sent party of 1 Officer and 50 O.Rs to the line to be attached to 'A' Coy for duty, also 1 Officer from 'B' Coy. 'A' Coy sent down enterprise party from LEFT FRONT to SUBSIDIARY LINE. During the day our artillery carried out destructive shoots on enemy wire and parapet of INCH TRENCH and wire I.31.d. Enemy artillery activity normal. At 1.40 p.m. 50 rds 10.5 cm shells on RAILWAY FARM and SUPPORT LINE I.27.a. and I.20.t. Trench mortars active. Enemy machine guns active during the night on ROAD behind SUBSIDIARY LINE (RATION FARM to DESOLANQUE FARM).	
		10.30 p.m.	Enemy searchlight swept NO MAN'S LAND I.26.3 - I.20.1. Patrol left our line at I.16.6. 10.17. at 9.5 p.m. to reconnoitre ground, wire, and approaches for laying of bangalore torpedoes, and to engage any enemy seen on known tracks in front of his wire. Enemy wire found to be broad banded concertina, about 15 yards from trench. Immediately in front of parapet another thick belt, composed of iron stakes and knife rests. No enemy encountered.	
	6th		A few gas shells fell about I.16.c. 05.60 about 12.30 a.m. to 1.45 a.m. Between 10.30 a.m. and 11.30 a.m. our artillery continued destructive shoot on INCH TRENCH and SUPPORT, both wire and parapet. Our Lewis Guns and the	

WAR DIARY or INTELLIGENCE SUMMARY

Army Form C. 2118.

Place	Date	Hour	Summary of Events and Information	Remarks and references to Appendices
	Nov 1917			
	6th		Artillery fired on gaps in enemy wire at intervals during the night. 2 enemy planes patrolled our FRONT LINE at 400km at about 1000 feet. One plane over SUBSIDIARY LINE and rear areas from 5.30 p.m. to 6.30 p.m. Our aerial activity below normal. Enemy machine guns very active during the night on road behind SUBSIDIARY LINE from RATION FARM to CHAPELLE. Patrol left our line to lie in wait for enemy patrol along track in front of his wire at I.16.d.50.70 to I.16.f.55.00. No enemy encountered.	
	7th		Our artillery continued destructive and wire cutting programme on INCH and INCLEMENT TRENCHES. Enemy artillery unusually quiet.	
	8th	1.24 a.m.	6 Bangalore Torpedoes were exploded in enemy wire I.16.d.50.80 to I.16.f.55.00. in conjunction with the operation carried out by the Special Coy REs, who fired 595 Gas IMs into WEZ MACQUART. Raiding party of 13th Bn Rifle Bde entered INCLEMENT TRENCH and found it unoccupied. (Detailed narrative attached). Our machine guns and IMs assisted in the operation. Many lights breaking into 4 or 5 red balls sent up opposite Right Batter. at dusk. Few lights breaking into strings of green sent up at 1.30 a.m. from WEZ MACQUART.	
		10 am - 2 p.m.	about 200 m/s 5.9s on I.8.d. Searching for new battery positions. Otherwise artillery was unusually quiet. IMs and MGs also very quiet. Three of our observation planes returning across our line at 12.15 p.m. were heavily engaged by hostile AA guns.	
		6.30 p.m.	one green light sent up from INCIDENT SUPPORT. No action observed.	

Army Form C. 2118.

WAR DIARY
or
INTELLIGENCE SUMMARY.
(Erase heading not required.)

Place	Date	Hour	Summary of Events and Information	Remarks and references to Appendices
	Nov 1917.			
	8th		Patrols out from dusk to dawn to watch gap. No wire enemy wire by Bangalore Torpedoes on previous night. No hostile party seen.	
	9th		Aerial activity above normal. Our planes over enemy line at 11.30 a.m., 12 noon, 2 p.m. At 3.30 p.m. heavily engaged by enemy A.A. fire. At 5 p.m. one of our machines returning across our line at a very low altitude was engaged by enemy M.G. fire, and fired back on enemy trenches on return.	
		9 p.m.	Special Cy. R.E's fired 608 Gas D.M's from 12"–4" D.M's as at about BURNT FARM. Firing continued until 9.16 p.m. The wind was mild, about 5 m/p/h, but was not in a favourable direction for the discharge of gas. The cloud could be distinctly seen travelling along NO MANS LAND in a North Easterly direction, and eventually passed over our front line and close support posts in the LEFT Company area I.15.d.25.00 to I.16.a.80.80. The sentries in these posts had time to warn the posts and get their helmets on. Our M.G's co-operated in the gas discharge.	
		9.17 p.m.	Enemy retaliated for gas bombardment with 5.9" H.E. and 77mm on SUPPORT and CLOSE SUPPORT LINE. RIGHT Company area. About 100 rds. in all. Retaliation on RUE DE BOIS and KNIGHTS BRIDGE with Heavy T.M's. Vernal M.G. fire on and behind SUBSIDIARY LINE. The enemy did not send up coloured lights during bombardment, but Very lights sounded immediately and continued ringing until about 9.25 p.m. Patrols kept the gap in enemy wire under close observation, but no enemy parties were observed. During the evening took over Right Half Bharra from 10th Bn C.E.P.	

CASUALTIES — O.Rs — 1 KILLED
  8 WOUNDED

A Co. in RIGHT FRONT
D : LEFT "
B : RIGHT RES }
C : LEFT " } Bharra BILLETS

WAR DIARY or INTELLIGENCE SUMMARY.

Army Form C. 2118.

(Erase heading not required.)

Place	Date	Hour	Summary of Events and Information	Remarks and references to Appendices
	Nov. 1917.			
	10th		Activity below normal all day. During the evening the 16th Bn was relieved in the LEFT SUBSECTOR BOIS GRENIER by the 13th Bn R.W. Fus. 2 Companies 16th R.W.F. remained in SUBSIDIARY LINE, attached to 13th R.W.Fus. The other 2 companies returned to BILLETS in ERQUINGHEM. Relief complete 8.5 p.m. Patrol went out to watch gap in enemy wire made by Bangalore Torpedoes. This patrol was taken over by the 13th Bn R.W.Fus.	
	11th		2/Lt. E.G. WILLIAMS transferred to and proceeded to join 1st Bn R.W.F. Supplied fatigue parties as called for in ERQUINGHEM. Standing Orders. Day devoted to cleaning up and inspection of kit. AWARDS. L/C A. WILLIAMS - MILITARY MEDAL Pte P. MAIDEN - DO -	
	12th 13th 14th		Supplied fatigue parties as above, and carried out training as per programme. During the evening of the 14th the 2 Companies from BILLETS in ERQUINGHEM relieved the 2 Companies in SUBSIDIARY LINE, the latter returning to BILLETS in ERQUINGHEM. CASUALTIES — WOUNDED — 3 O.R.	
	15th 16th		Carried out training as per programme, and supplied fatigue parties as above. During evening of 16th the 16th Bn R.W.F. relieved the 13th Bn R.W.F. in the LEFT SUBSECTION BOIS GRENIER as under:- A Coy from RIGHT RES to RIGHT FRONT D " " LEFT " to CENTRE RES. C " " BILLETS to LEFT FRONT B " " " to CENTRE FRONT. Relief complete 8 p.m.	

Army Form C. 2118.

WAR DIARY
or
INTELLIGENCE SUMMARY.
(Erase heading not required.)

Instructions regarding War Diaries and Intelligence Summaries are contained in F. S. Regs., Part II. and the Staff Manual respectively. Title pages will be prepared in manuscript.

Place	Date	Hour	Summary of Events and Information	Remarks and references to Appendices
	Nov 1917			
	17th	7am-8am	Our 18 pdrs firing on rear areas and must. 9.30 am 18 pdrs retaliated on enemy minnie' positions. 9.30am - 10.50 am enemy artillery retaliated on own support areas from FM DE BIEZ to BURNT FM. 10.30-11 am Gas shells in ARMENTIERS. Enemy shelled our own in front of post I.16.C.65.85. from 5pm to 5.40 pm with 77mm. Enemy 2Ms very active. Three of our patrols went out during the night.	
	18th		During the day enemy and our own artillery & 2Ms very active.	
		2 pm	one of our 9.45" fired 15 rds all of which fell short in NO MANS LAND. Aerial activity above normal. During the night a land mine was laid on track in front of enemy wire at INCH TRENCH by REs, covered by our patrols. Three patrols were out during the night watching this trap.	
		5.15 pm	"27" Red rockets sent up opposite this sector, mostly from SUPPORT and RESERVE lines no action followed. REINFORCEMENTS - O.R. - 43	
	19th		Artillery and MGs active all day. At 2pm and 4pm enemy shelled junction of WELLINGTON AV. and SUBSIDIARY LINE with 4.2s. 1 direct hit on Bn. Hdqr. (I.14.d.50.6.) During the night one of our patrols located strong enemy wiring party at I.16.d.45.70. Artillery fire was called for and this party was dispersed with 30 rds. Enemy MGs opposite this sector noticeably quieter. REINFORCEMENTS - OFFICER - 2/Lt J. RICHARDS.	
	20th		Several trans during the day enemy 2Ms opened fire; on own 18pdrs retaliating on known 2M positions. During the night the 2Ms ceased fire alto' a few rounds Aircraft inactive. During the night 4 patrols went out to watch land mine	

Army Form C. 2118

WAR DIARY
or
INTELLIGENCE SUMMARY
(Erase heading not required.)

Instructions regarding War Diaries and Intelligence Summaries are contained in F. S. Regs., Part II. and the Staff Manual respectively. Title Pages will be prepared in manuscript.

Place	Date	Hour	Summary of Events and Information	Remarks and references to Appendices
	Nov 1917.			
	21st		Activity normal. From 1–3.0 p.m. 6" Newton Guns fired on I.22.a.40.62 and I.22.b.62.78. Our artillery carried out covering fire to this shoot. During the night enemy MGs fired bursts of enfilade fire over CATHRINE I.21.a.70.85. Our listening patrols left our line to watch land mine at I.16.d.45.95.	
	22nd		Owing to poor visibility there was very little activity during the day. In the evening the Battn. was relieved by the 13th Bn.R.W.F. Two Companies and Headquarters returned to BILLETS in ERQUINGHEM, the other two Coys remained in the Subsidiary Line, attached to 13th R.W.F. Supplied fatigue parties as called for in Standing Orders and carried out training as per programme.	
	23rd		During the evening the two companies in Subsidiary line were relieved by the 13th Bn.R.W.F. and proceeded to BILLETS in ERQUINGHEM. Carried out training as per programme and supplied fatigue parties as above. On the 24th MAJOR S.L. HUNKIN, D.S.O., assumed command of the Battn. vice LT.COL. H.F.N. JOURDAIN, C.M.G., to ENGLAND.	
	24th / 28th		During night of 28th the Battn. relieved the 13th Bn.R.W.F. in the LEFT SUB-SECTOR BOIS GRENIER, CENTRE and LEFT FRONT Coy areas. Two Companies in Subsidiary Line. The RIGHT FRONT Coy being held by 17th Bn.C.E.P. Relief complete 7.55 p.m. Patrol sent out to watch land mine on track in front of enemy wire	

Army Form C. 2118.

WAR DIARY
or
INTELLIGENCE SUMMARY.
(Erase heading not required.)

Instructions regarding War Diaries and Intelligence Summaries are contained in F.S. Regs., Part II. and the Staff Manual respectively. Title pages will be prepared in manuscript.

Place	Date	Hour	Summary of Events and Information	Remarks and references to Appendices
	Nov. 1917. 29th		Enemy activity normal during the day. At 10.30 am an enemy plane driven down out of control, falling in WEZ MACQUART.	
		2.30 pm	Our 6" Newton trench mortars carried out shoot on enemy wire at I.16.d.52.9½.	
		3 pm	One Coy from SUBSIDIARY LINE commenced to relieve Coy of 19th Bn C.E.P. on RIGHT FRONT. Coy of 17th Bn C.E.P. remained in SUBSIDIARY LINE until 4.30 pm and then proceeded to BILLETS in ERQUINGHEM.	
		11.10 pm – 11.30 pm	Enemy put a Heavy T.M. barrage on RIGHT BATTN FRONT. 10 LTMs fell on I.20.d.95.75 and I.20.d.50.70 neither fork was damaged. During the barrage enemy MGs were firing recon our front. During the rest of the night MG fire was normal. Patrols out watching landmine.	
			CASUALTIES – OFFICER – WOUNDED – 2/LT. WILLIAM OWEN.	
	30th	8.30 – 9.15 am	40 5.9s and 4.2s in CHAPELLE D'ARMENTIERS and Subsidiary Line I.9.c.25.40. 3 pm – 4 pm 20 4.2s on SIGNAL BOX and I.14.d.50.90.	
		2.40 – 4 pm	Our TMs carried out shoot on I.21.d.40.70 and encountercated on ORCHARD and WINE AV. I.15.C. with 20 77s, also 12 Medium TMs on I.16.d.20.70.	
		9.45 pm	18 pdrs opened burst of shrapnel on enemy working party located by patrol at I.21.c.92.75. Men quiet. Landmine watched by patrols during the night.	

J. Neu Rin Major.
Commanding, 16th Bn R.W. Fusiliers.

SECRET.   16th Batt. R.W.Fusiliers.
                                                    C. 115.

TO:-
    113th Infantry Brigade.

        After preliminary Orders had been given out with
reference to the Placing and Firing of 6 Bangalore Torpedoes
in the enemy's line on the night of the 7/8th November 1917-
and after receiving Orders from Headquarters,113th Infantry
Brigade- the following Orders were promulgated on the 7th
November 1917:-

" TO:-
    O.C. "A" Coy, 16th R.W.F.
    O.C. "D" Coy,   do

            Reference:- Map BOIS GRENIER Section 36N.W.4,1/10,000.

1. Today, ZERO to be notified later, a party of the 16th R.W.Fus
   will fire fire 6 Bangalore Torpedoes which will be laid in the
   enemy's wire between I.16.d.45.88 and I.16.b.55.00.

2. The party will consist of 2 Officers, 4 N.C.O's and 30 O.R.,
   of the 16th Batt.R.W.Fus, and 1 N.C.O. and 2 O.R. of the 123rd
   Field Company R.E., the whole under the Command of 2/Lieut.
   V.P.WILLIAMS, 16th Batt.R.W.Fusiliers.

3. The time table of Operations will be :-

   ZERO minus 2 hours.   Party leaves our lines and proceeds towards
                         German trenches.

   ZERO minus 35 mins.   Bangalore Torpedoes will all be laid in the
                         wire and connected up.

   ZERO minus 20 mins.   Party will withdraw 200 yards from the
                         German wire.

   ZERO.   Torpedoes will be fired.

   ZERO plus (as convenient). Party will withdraw to our own line.

4. Officer Commanding Party will see that there are duplicate
   methods of firing the torpedoes. In the event of the torpedoes
   failing to go off at the ordered time the party will find out
   what is wrong, remedy the defect and fire the torpedoes as soon
   as possible. In the event of a continued failure, the party will
   withdraw to our line the torpedoes that fail to explode.

5. LEITH WALK will be used by the party both for coming and going.

6. Officer Commanding "A" Company will establish a report centre
   at EUNICE POST, I.16.a.65.53.

7. (a) No 1 Special Company R.E. will discharge Gas at ZERO Hour.

   (b) In the event of the wind being unfavourable for this discharge, the following message will be sent to all recipients
   of this Order:-

       "Reference this Brigade Order No 165. CHICAGO."

   All Front Line Posts on Left and Centre Battalion fronts will
   wear Box Respirators from ZERO minus 5 to ZERO plus 15.

2.

8. Watches will be synchronized at this Batt.Headquarters at 6 p.m. today.

   2/Lieut V.P.WILLIAMS or 2/Lieut F.T.LINTON will attend."

7/11/17."

After a careful Inspection of all Stores, and of the Arms and Equipment of all men employed on the Raid.

NARRATIVE. At 10.24 p.m. on the evening of the 7th November, the carrying party left with 6 Bangalore torpedoes and all material, and proceeding by the SUBSIDIARY LINE, and LILLE ROAD, reached EILEEN POST at about 10.50 p.m.

The Covering Parties were armed with Rifle, Bayonet and 2 Bombs. The Laying Parties had only 2 Bombs, one in each side pocket.

At 11.24 p.m., the Covering Parties left our lines and proceeded to their allotted positions under the guidance of 2/Lieut V.P.WILLIAMS. The Laying Party followed shortly afterwards and was led by 2/Lieut F.T.LINTON, 18th Batt.R.W.Fus, who, with SAPPER, TOTTEY, carried the leads and proceeded directly towards the enemy's line. From the outset this party had to repair frequent breakages in the leads, which were torn by our own wire, which was quite unavoidable. These breaks were repaired at once and 2/Lieut F.T.LINTON and Sappers TOTTEY and JONES were indefatigable in their efforts in this respect. This party had to repair 15 breakages in the leads before reaching the German wire, and the time spent out this Operation was one hour and a half. The Laying Party, however, reached the German line at 12.54 a.m., and the Torpedoes were at once got into position and the leads connected up, and all was in readiness for the return of the Parties. The actual linking up of the leads and the final adjustment of the Six Torpedoes took exactly 13 minutes, and all was ready at 1.7 a.m.

The party under 2/Lieut F.T.LINTON left the German Lines at this hour, and on examining the leads on the return journey, another break was found and mended about 150 yards from our own lines. The greatest trouble was spent by all the men to make the Scheme a success.

The enemy brought up a Machine Gun between the two belts of wire, opposite the left covering party at 11.50 p.m., and this Gun fired intermittently, with certain stoppages, until 12.30 a.m. The position of this Gun was at I.16.d.54.99. There was another hostile Machine Gun located at I.16.d.54.87. which fired several bursts at about midnight, but was silent afterwards. One Sniper fired at 12.25 a.m. and only narrowly missed the foremost members of the Laying Party, this Sniper was located at I.16.d.53.93. There was, however, no hesitation or delay. The Torpedoes were laid exactly at 15 feet intervals, and the area breached by the explosion was from I.16.d.51.90 to I.16.d.50.83.

The last repair was completed and the circuit was tested, and the Covering Parties were drawn back from the Germans about the space of 100 yards at ZERO hour exactly, and at eight seconds after ZERO hour (1.24 a.m) the exploder was put into force from a position at I.16.a.85.27., and the explosion was successful. This was wired back to Headquarters and was received at 1.30 a.m.

All parties withdrew at once, and the Operation was completed in every detail. There were no casualties in the party, and although the Machine Gun fire harassed the Covering Parties very much, all men behaved with ~~considerable~~ pluck and determination and shewed a coolness throughout the Operation.

The following Officers and N.C.O's and men behaved with great gallantry and worked indefatigably towards the success of the Scheme:-

    2/Lieut V.P.WILLIAMS.   16th Batt. R.W.Fusiliers.
    2/Lieut.F.T.LINTON.   16th Batt. R.W.Fusiliers.
    No. 15389. Cpl.J.ROBERTS.   16th Batt. R.W.Fusiliers.
    No. 6489. Pte.F.GRIST.   16th Batt. R.W.Fusiliers.

-:and:-
    No 446238. Sapper J.TOTTEY. No 4 Sect.123 Field Coy R.E.
    No 82507. do G.T.JONES. do

who worked splendidly out on Patrol, and to whom with 2/Lieut F.T.LINTON, CPL. J.ROBERTS and PTE. GRIST, the success of the enterprise is mainly due. 2/Lieut V.P.WILLIAMS took a great amount of trouble in organizing the Raid, and his arrangements worked very well.

Both the Officers employed on the Operation did exceedingly well, and I desire to bring to notice the names of the two Sappers mentioned above. No praise is too good for these two men.

Gas was also discharged from our lines also at ZERO hour.

                                          Lieut Col.,
8th Novr.1917.   Commanding, 16th Batt.R.W.Fus.

16th Batt. ROYAL WELSH FUSILIERS

Vol 25

WAR DIARY

for

DECEMBER 1917

25 F.
8 sheets

Army Form C. 2118.

WAR DIARY
for
INTELLIGENCE SUMMARY.
(Erase heading not required.)

November 1917.

Instructions regarding War Diaries and Intelligence Summaries are contained in F.S. Regs., Part II. and the Staff Manual respectively. Title pages will be prepared in manuscript.

Place	Date	Hour	Summary of Events and Information	Remarks and references to Appendices
BOIS-GRENIER LEFT SECTOR	1.		The Battalion holding the Left Subsection BOIS GRENIER Disposition as follows :- 3 Companies in front line and one in support.	
	"	8.30am	One of our Stokes Mortars are Enemy Artillery fired Machine Gun into German trenches RIGHT Enemy Company front and support line during the day, but at 6.10pm shelled RIGHT Coy. line heavily after an to 3 Red lights sent up from Enemy line E.21.a. in answer Coy. Rocket was fired from AUDREY Post. No damage done. Hostile Machine Guns active during early evening 2 patrols sent out during the night, one took at 1.21.c 92.80 found 10 to 20 Plram recently cleared.	
	2.		Activity below normal all day. During the night enemy fired bursts on road behind SUBSIDIARY Line.	
	3.	1/2pm	Our 6" M.L.Gs. fired 50 rounds on enemy gun pits about 1.22.a.45.79 considerable damage reported. Our Artillery co-operated with covering fire to M.Gs. also fired in retaliation to Enemy M.Gs. firing on INDEX trench SUPPORT and INCREASE trench. Enemy retaliated on F.L. Shoot with 10.5 cms. Opened the ORCHARD I.15.c. The 13"/13" Bn. R.W.Fusiliers relieved the 16th (S) Bn. R.W.Fusiliers in LEFT SUBSECTION, relief complete 6.25 pm. On relief "A" and "B" Companies 16th R.W. marched to Huts at LA ROLANDERIE, "C" and "D" and H.Qrs. Companies returned to Billets in ERQUINGHEM.	
RESERVE			Supplied Fatigue Parties as called for in "ERQUINGHEM Standing Orders"	

Army Form C. 2118.

WAR DIARY
INTELLIGENCE SUMMARY.
(Erase heading not required.)

Place	Date	Hour	Summary of Events and Information	Remarks and references to Appendices
RESERVE	4/6/7		also Training carried out as per Programme rendered. Lieut-Col. E.J. de P. O'KELLY assumed command of Battalion on 5th.	
LEFT SUBSECTION BOIS GRENIER	7		During the evening of the 7th the Battalion relieved the 13th (S) Bn Rif. Rgt. in the LEFT Subsectn BOIS GRENIER. Relief Complete 7.35 p.m. Disposition - 3 Companies in front line and 1 Company in Support. Enemy M.G's active at intervals during the night. 2 Patrols sent out to watch Land Mine.	
	8.	1 a.m.	Our Artillery carried out shoot on INCENSE AVENUE according to Programme.	
		1.30 & 2.30 a.m.	77's on ORCHARD (I.15.a) and I.14.d. also 14 - 77's on COWGATE I.15.b.	
		2.64 a.m.	36 L.T. M.b's in I.16.a. 80.90. Patrols sent out to watch Land mine.	
			Night unusually quiet.	
	9.	8.15 a.m.	Land mine at I.16.d. 50.90 reported to have exploded. Patrol sent out at 4.15 p.m. to verify this, and to obtain identification.	
		4.15 p.m.	Patrols about NO MANS LAND report finding from 10 indicals that the mine had exploded. Our Artillery put down Barrage on INCH Farm I.16.d.	
		5.25 p.m.	Enemy patrol seen and fired on by garrison of AUDREY NIGHT POST 4.30 - 5.15 p.m. (I.21.a. 65.05). Patrol went out immediately to reconnoitre and secure identifications, but failed to get any.	
	10.	6.6 & 7 a.m.	Heavy Bombardment of RIGHT Battalion which spread to our trenches. Violence damage at several points. No battle and mist enemy and no casualties. Artillery quiet throughout remainder of the day. Enemy T.M's normally active. Hostile planes very active during the afternoon, especially over RIGHT Company front. 2 Patrols sent out during the night.	

CASUALTIES - REINFORCEMENTS. Other Ranks.
KILLED (on Patrol) 1 O.R. 40.

WAR DIARY / INTELLIGENCE SUMMARY

Army Form C. 2118.

Place	Date	Hour	Summary of Events and Information	Remarks and references to Appendices
LEFT SUB-SECTION BOIS GRENIER	11		During the morning our Artillery fired in retaliation on hostile T.M. positions.	
		2.5/6 3 p.m.	9.45" T.M's fired 58 rounds on wire I.16.b.70.05. and 3" Stokes retaliated to enemy T.M.'s firing 50 rounds on INCLINE INCLUDE and INCLUDE Support trenches.	
		12.45 a.m.	Two of our planes dropped 2 bombs near SNIPERS HOUSE I.22.a. During the evening the Battalion in LEFT subsection BOIS GRENIER Relief complete by 13th(S) Bn. R.W. Fus. 16th(S) Bn. R.W. Fus. on relief remained in Support Battalion Area vacated by 15th(S) Bn. R.W. Fus. Disposition 3 Companies along SUBSIDIARY LINE. 1 Company at QUATRE CHEMINS.	
			CASUALTIES. - WOUNDED. 1 O.R.	
SUPPORT AREA	12 13 14 15		Indoor working parties according to table. "Rest" Company at QUATRE CHEMINS being changed daily to have a rest. Rain etc.	
LEFT SUBSECTION BOIS GRENIER	16		During the evening of the 16th the Battalion relieved the 15th(S) Bn. R.W. Fus. in LEFT subsection BOIS GRENIER. Relief complete 6.35 p.m. 2 Patrols sent out.	
		3.15 a.m.	12 Heavy T.M's on AUDREY I.21.a.7.1. and I.21.a.6.3. Our T.M.'s carried out a shoot to which the enemy retaliated with 12 H. T.M's on I.21.a.80.10. 30 L.T.M/s on I.20.b. 60.30. 10. 25 a.m. 2 Patrols sent out.	
		Dawn	Our T.M.'s on I.21.a. 80.10 to I.16.a. 05.60 and again at 1.30 p.m.	
	17	9 am	3" Stokes Gun retaliated on "Pineapples" on SALOP Area. Activity below normal all day.	
		3.15 p.m.	5 Enemy planes flying low over Battalion Area	
		5.15 p.m.	3 "Green" lights opposite PEAR TREE FARM. No attained action followed. Fighting patrol and covering party sent out during the night. No identifications secured.	

WAR DIARY
INTELLIGENCE SUMMARY

Army Form C. 2118.

Place	Date	Hour	Summary of Events and Information	Remarks and references to Appendices
BOIS GRENIER	18		Activity below normal all day. 10.45a.m. 1 Enemy Plane over LEFT Subsection driven off by A.A. Aircraft fire. During the morning enemy plane ranging on Signal line EAST of WEZ MACQUART. 2 Patrols sent out during the night, also Covering Party.	
	19.		Artillery Activity below normal all day. Visibility very poor. Patrols sent out during the night to watch and ascertain any Enemy Working or Wiring Parties, and secure identifications, but failed to find any. CASUALTIES. WOUNDED 1. Other Rank. REINFORCEMENTS – OFFICERS ONE – 2/Lt. G.W. CARR.	
	20.		No Artillery or Aerial activity. Visibility very poor. The 16th (S) Bn Northumberland were relieved by the 11th Bat Australian Infantry. Relief complete 9.30 a.m. on relief the Battalion moved into 6 RESERVE Billets in FLEURBAIX Sector H.O.Sqrs at H. 21. a. 30. 20. Company Billets situated far between	
FLEURBAIX RESERVE	21		Battalion in Reserve. Day devoted to cleaning up and resting. DECREASE Officers – 2/Lt. S.G. YOUNG struck off strength and taken on strength of VIIIth Corps.	
	22.		Battalion in Reserve. Carried out during the morning training. Declaration of Chirolines Denies by 3 Companies CASUALTIES (accidently) WOUNDED – 1 Other Rank.	
	23.		Working Party of 5 Officers and 250 O.Rs supplied by the Batt on this Burying Reconnoissance carried out during the day of new Battalion Front	

WAR DIARY or INTELLIGENCE SUMMARY

Army Form C. 2118.

Place	Date	Hour	Summary of Events and Information	Remarks and references to Appendices
	24.		Working Parties of 4 Officers and 200 other ranks supplied by the Battalion to Bde. Siege Co. yesterday, from 8.30 a.m. to 12 noon. Moved off from Billets at FLEURBAIX. Relieved the 15 K.R. and took over in the RIGHT Sub-Section FLEURBAIX. Relief complete 5.30 p.m. disposition - 2 Companies in front line and 2 Companies in SUPPORT. Headquarters WYE FARM H.35.b.85.15.	
	25.	5-9 p.m.	T.M. Shoot carried out as arranged. Double retaliation for our shoot. Reconnoitring Patrol of 1 N.C.O. and 6 O.R's sent out from 8 to 9 p.m. from RICHARD POST to reconnoitre enemy wire in front of our Salient between RICHARD POST and ABBOTS LANE. Wire found to be very weak and bent forming no obstacle. Old Sap also in front of Salient badly knocked about.	
	25.		T.M's carried out short shoot on enemy Knaggsone point to assist an Artillery Battalion Tank. No activity except rifle patrol sent out during the night. No identifications secured.	
	26.	10.30 a.m.	6 "Pineapple" Grenades on N.5.a.60.10	
		10.45 a.m.	2, 10.5 on GUNNERS WALK H36.d.30.40. REINFORCEMENTS 3 other ranks. CASUALTIES - WOUNDED 1 O.R.	
			Patrol sent out from 7.15 to 8.15 p.m. No identifications by the enemy. No identifications. Patrol abatted and fired on CASUALTIES - 2 KILLED - WOUNDED - 1 other ranks	
		11 p.m.	Enemy Red Rocket went up in our own night. No action reported. A large dog was seen from RICHARD POST to come from enemy's lines into NO MANS LAND. After running about for a short time [illegible]	

Army Form C. 2118.

WAR DIARY
INTELLIGENCE SUMMARY.
(Erase heading not required.)

Instructions regarding War Diaries and Intelligence Summaries are contained in F.S. Regs., Part II. and the Staff Manual respectively. Title pages will be prepared in manuscript.

Place	Date	Hour	Summary of Events and Information	Remarks and references to Appendices
RIGHT SUBSECTION FLEURBAIX.	27th.		Day and night relatively quiet. No activity whatever. Intel Company Relief took place and then the Battalion Reconnoitring Patrol of 1 N.C.O. and 5 O.R's went out at 8pm. No identifications secured or any casualties incurred.	
	28th.		No activity during the day or night. Supplied reconnoitring Patrol of 1 N.C.O. and 5 O.R's to examine wire between RICHARD and ROBERT POSTS; found to be very weak.	
	29th.	2.15th 2.30pm	Ration party killed by barrage during the morning. 20 "Rifle" Grenades fired in "J." Post and vicinity of junction of ABBOTS LANE and SUPPORT Line. 3" Stokes Guns fired in retaliation 6 rounds "Pineapple" Grenades on ABBOTS LANE. - 15 rounds fired into enemy trenches.	
	30th.	10.30 am 1.30— 2.30pm 2.30pm	6 ½ 12 "Pineapple" on ABBOTS LANE. 1 No. 6" carried out shoot as per programme. 6 "Pineapples" on BAY AVENUE H.36.d.65.75. CASUALTIES:- WOUNDED- 2. other ranks. Intel Company Relief carried out within the Battalion sent out during the night. No identification secured. Night otherwise quiet.	
	31st.	12 noon 4.45 pm 12 pm	8 - 1¾lbs fired on H.36.c.40.10. 2. 1¾lbs fired on H.36.c.40.10. 6 "Pineapple" Grenades fired round "JAY" POST. H36.c.50.10.	

Army Form C. 2118.

WAR DIARY
INTELLIGENCE SUMMARY
(Erase heading not required.)

Instructions regarding War Diaries and Intelligence Summaries are contained in F.S. Regs., Part II. and the Staff Manual respectively. Title pages will be prepared in manuscript.

Place	Date	Hour	Summary of Events and Information	Remarks and references to Appendices
RIGHT SUBSECTION FLEURBAIX	31st	7.30 (?)	Red Rocket fired from N.6.c.50.45. No action afterwards. Nothing happened.	
			Shoot by Left Group – 38th Divisional Artillery at 12 midnight. 2 Patrols sent out during the night – one of which was fired upon at ----- spot near of A Happy New Year came from the Germans. Nothing occurred but by Companies reported to thicken the wire in front of own line and Posts.	

Stanfully
Lieut. Col. [?]
Commanding 16th (S) Batt. R. Fusiliers

1st January 1918.

16th Batt. ROYAL WELSH FUSILIERS
Vol 26
WAR DIARY
FOR
JANUARY 1918.

Army Form C. 2118.

16th (S) Bn Royal Welsh Fusiliers
113th Infantry Brigade
38th (Welsh) Division

WAR DIARY
or
INTELLIGENCE SUMMARY.
(Erase heading not required.)

Instructions regarding War Diaries and Intelligence Summaries are contained in F. S. Regs., Part II. and the Staff Manual respectively. Title pages will be prepared in manuscript.

Place	Date	Hour	Summary of Events and Information	Remarks and references to Appendices
	1918. January 1st		No artillery activity during the morning. In the afternoon shots carried out by Left Group 38th Divn. Artillery. 6" Newton Guns cutting wire in front of INDEX TRENCH, covering fire by 9/121 Bty. on enemy O.Ps CHOCOLATE HOUSE (O.13.d.00.80) and along INDEX SUPPORT. 2 reconnoitring patrols sent out during the night. The two front line bays carried out wiring.	
	2nd		Same amount of artillery activity during the day, but owing to poor visibility there was no aerial activity. During the afternoon and evening the two Companies in Support relieved the two front line Companies. Wiring carried out by the two Coys in front line during the night. Two reconnaissance patrols sent out. Enemy appeared nervous, fired numerous Very lights. Enemy machine guns more active than usual during the night.	
	3rd		Artillery active during the day, fired a burst on INCREASE TRENCH and SUPPORT at 6.45pm. Trench also fired during the day. Enemy artillery also fairly active. Aircraft on both sides busy on observation and patrol work. Enemy M.Gs very active during the early part of the night. Two patrols sent out during the night to patrol the ground between following points O.1.a.07.80 — I.31.c.31.20. No enemy patrols or working parties were heard.	

Army Form C. 2118.

WAR DIARY
or
INTELLIGENCE SUMMARY.

(Erase heading not required.)

Instructions regarding War Diaries and Intelligence Summaries are contained in F. S. Regs., Part II. and the Staff Manual respectively. Title pages will be prepared in manuscript.

Place	Date	Hour	Summary of Events and Information	Remarks and references to Appendices
	Jan 18. 4th		Our artillery quiet during the morning. 2.15 p.m. – 2.50 p.m. and 4 p.m. shelled INDEX TRENCH and SUPPT. 3.16 p.m. rapid burst on INCREASE SUPPT. 4 p.m. active 2 M.G. silenced at O.1.6.26.70. Enemy carried out intermittent fire on roads behind Left and Centre Subsections. Aircraft very active, and enemy M.G. guns engaged on A.A. work. Two reconnoitring patrols out during the night, but no enemy patrols or working parties engaged.	
	5th		Very little activity owing to poor visibility. 3" Stokes guns fired 99 rds on INDEX SUPPT and NEAR SUPPT in retaliation to enemy trench M.G. 13th Bn R.W.F. relieved 16th R.W.F. in the Right Subsection, relief complete 9.55 p.m. Battn moved to BILLETS in FLEURBAIX.	
	6th – 8th		Battn in Reserve. Wiring carried out at LAVESSEE.	
	9th		The Battn relieved the 13th Bn R.W.F. in the Right Subsection. Relief complete 7 p.m. Patrol out during the night, but no enemy seen or heard.	
	10th		10.0 a.m. Pineapple grenades on front and support lines. Our own T.M's retaliating. Enemy replied with 10 77's ovars area N.6a. 11.30 a.m. 10 77's and 5 4.2.0 on junction of BAY AVENUE and HUDSONS BAY. 2 patrols sent out, but no enemy engaged.	

WAR DIARY
or
INTELLIGENCE SUMMARY.

(Erase heading not required.)

Army Form C. 2118.

Place	Date	Hour	Summary of Events and Information	Remarks and references to Appendices
	Jan 18			
	11th		Aircraft inactive throughout the day. Artillery fairly quiet, at 2.35 pm an enemy T.M. was silenced at O.1.k.26.70. Enemy M.Gs very active in the early part of night and fired few bursts afterwards. 2 patrols sent out during the night.	
	12th		Our amount of aerial activity during the day. 6 enemy planes flying over our lines by front at 1.30 pm. Fighting patrol sent out during the night. 2 patrols between points N.6.c.76.96 and N.6.c.40.10 from midnight to 2. am.	
	13th		Artillery quiet, but aircraft fairly active, otherwise quiet. 2 patrols sent out during the night.	
	14th		Our aircraft very active during the morning, owing to poor visibility artillery and aircraft were inactive during the afternoon. The Battn was relieved by the 6th Bn Royal West Kent Regt during the night. Relief complete about 10 pm. Battn moved to BILLETS in SAILLY	
	15th		Battn moved from SAILLY by march route to the MERVILLE AREA, arrived BILLETS about 2.15 pm.	
	16th		Day devoted to cleaning up. No training carried out.	

WAR DIARY
or
INTELLIGENCE SUMMARY.

Army Form C. 2118.

Place	Date	Hour	Summary of Events and Information	Remarks and references to Appendices
	Jany '18 17th to 31st		Carried out Training in the MERVILLE AREA as per programme issued, also supplied working parties for construction of miniature range. REINFORCEMENTS. OFFICERS. 9th — Do — 2/Lt. W.G. LLOYD 18th — Do — 2/Lt. R.W. THOMAS 19th — Do — 2/Lt. B.O. DAVIES 20th — Do — O.RANKS. 24th — Do — 6. 30th — Do — 4. 6. During the period the Bn was in the line the weather was very cold, and on the day of relief a heavy fall of snow made marching difficult. This was followed by thaw on the following day, and the march from SAILLY to MERVILLE and was almost continuous. For several days the MERVILLE AREA was flooded, many of the roads being almost impassable. Limbers were employed to convey troops over the flooded parts.	

A.D. Hunkin Major,
Commanding 16th (S) Ankht

Vol 27

27 F.
6 sheets

War Diary

16th Battn. Royal Welsh Fusiliers

February 1918

Instructions regarding War Diaries and Intelligence
Summaries are contained in F. S. Regs. Part II.
and the Staff Manual respectively. Title   pages
will be prepared in manuscript.

WAR DIARY
or
INTELLIGENCE SUMMARY.
(Erase heading not required.)

Army Form C. 2118.

16th (S) Bn Royal Welsh Fusiliers
113th Infantry Brigade
38th (Welsh) Division

February 1918

Place	Date	Hour	Summary of Events and Information	Remarks and references to Appendices
	1918 Feby 1st		Battalion occupying BILLETS in ARREWAGE (MERVILLE AREA).	
	2nd		Proceeded by march route to BILLETS at LA PIERRIERE (GUARBESQUE AREA) arriving BILLETS 3 p.m.	
	3/12		Marched to BILLETS at BOURECQ (ST. HILAIRE AREA) Arrived BILLETS 11 a.m. Training and Recreational training carried out as per programmes. Battalion was successful in several inter-Battn. competitions:— "A" Coy Cross Country Run. Musketry and several items of Transport. REINFORCEMENTS — OFFICERS 10. O. RANKS — 152.	
	13th		Battalion parade 9.30 a.m and proceeded by march route to LA PIERRIERE (GAURBESQUE AREA) arrived BILLETS at noon.	
	14th		Proceeded by march route to BILLETS in ESTAIRES, arriving at 3.30 p.m.	
	15th		Marched to the LAUNDRIES, and relieved the 2/4 SOUTH LANCASHIRE REGT in SUPPORT AREA, CENTRE SECTOR (ARMENTIERES). DISPOSITIONS :— Battn. N.Q.s, A, C (less 2 platoons) and D Coy at the LAUNDRIES H.S. in 45.70. B Coy at ASYLUM 2 Platoons "C" Coy in SUBSP. LINE under Command O.C. 13th R.W.F	

WAR DIARY or INTELLIGENCE SUMMARY

Army Form C. 2118.

(Erase heading not required.)

Instructions regarding War Diaries and Intelligence Summaries are contained in F. S. Regs., Part II. and the Staff Manual respectively. Title pages will be prepared in manuscript.

Place	Date	Hour	Summary of Events and Information	Remarks and references to Appendices
	Feby 18/18		Carried out training and supplied working party.	
	19.	8.40 p.m.	Relieved the 13th Bn R.W.F. in the FRONT LINE, ARMENTIERES SECTOR. Relief complete. DISPOSITIONS:— A. Coy RIGHT FRONT. D. Coy LEFT FRONT. B. " SUPPT. C. Coy " SUPPT. 16th Bn R.W.F. relieved in SUPPORT by 14th Bn R.W.F. 2 Patrols sent out during the night.	
	20.		Visibility very poor during the day. Artillery and T.M's quiet. Enemy snipers active during the morning on I.9.4 and FORT EGAL C.T. Our snipers claim victim at I.11.a.10.60. Aerial activity — nil.	
		6.25 p.m – 6.45 p.m.	Enemy bombarded our FRONT and SUPPORT LINES in I.5.a and c. with 5.9, 4.2 and H.T.M's. Our 18 pdrs retaliated on INANE TRENCH and SUPPORT with about 40 rds. Machine Guns Lewis active during the night.	
		6.45 p.m	Enemy sent up lights breaking into a little green from SUPPORT LINE. Apparently signal for bombardment to cease. 2 Patrols out during night to reconnoitre NO MANS LAND.	

Army Form C. 2118.

WAR DIARY
or
INTELLIGENCE SUMMARY.
(Erase heading not required.)

Instructions regarding War Diaries and Intelligence Summaries are contained in F.S. Regs., Part II. and the Staff Manual respectively. Title pages will be prepared in manuscript.

Place	Date	Hour	Summary of Events and Information	Remarks and references to Appendices
	21.		Visibility good throughout the day. Enemy shewed parties of artillery fire on posts 5, 6, 29, and 30 (I.5.a and c) and registering on PLANK AVE I.4.b between 10 am and 12 noon.	
			Our howvers fired on track areas throughout the day, and registered on LA HOUGRIE FME at 1 p.m.	
		11.50 a.m	Flight of 7 E.As. over our lines, and were engaged by A.A. and M.G. fire. One brought down opposite Right Brigade front.	
			Our aircraft active throughout the day.	
		5.45 p.m.	Hostile 2 M.Gs. fired 11 rds nw PLANK AVE. (I.4.b)	
			3 patrols out during the night to reconnoitre ditches in NO MAN'S LAND. Enemy M.Gs. too active during the night.	
	22.		Enemy 2 M.Gs. active during the day, chiefly on Posts Nos. 22 and 23. (I.5.c. 45.80. and I.5.c. 05.50.) to which our artillery retaliated on trenches C.29.d. I.11.a, and I.5.b, also on T.M. position I.5.t. 50 50, silencing it.	
			Our 2 M.Gs inactive. Aerial activity nil. Our snipers obtained victims at I.5.c. 80.15. at 6.50 a.m.	
			An Officer's patrol reconnoitred NO MAN'S LAND and gap between posts 4 and 5 (I.5.a.) from 6 p.m to 8.30 p.m. No enemy seen or heard.	
			CASUALTIES – O.R. 3. WOUNDED	

Army Form C. 2118.

WAR DIARY
or
INTELLIGENCE SUMMARY.
(Erase heading not required.)

Place	Date	Hour	Summary of Events and Information	Remarks and references to Appendices
	Feby 23rd	10 am/1 pm	Shelling DISTILLERY (I.4.a.50.90) and 1.15 p.m. 12 and 77 mm on Dump and Railway I.9.F.25.98, 10 of which were 'duds'.	
		3.15 p.m.	3 cm's Bye Shell on ARMENTIERES. 1.55 pm - 2.15 pm 30 L.T.Ms on FRONT and SUPPT. LINES, to which our artillery retaliated on INCARNATE and INCANDESCENT TRENCHES.	
			3 Patrols left our lines at I.11.a.06.80 to lie in wait for suspected enemy raiding party on No. 4 Post. No movement of enemy seen or heard. Battalion relieved in the FRONT LINE by 14th Bn.R.W.R. Relief complete 9.6 p.m.	
			Moved into Reserve BILLETS at ERQUINGHEM.	
	24/2/		Carried out training as per programme, and supplied working parties as called for on working party table.	
	27th		Battalion relieved in the RESERVE AREA by the 14th Bn.R.W.R. Relieved 13th Bn. R.W.R. in SUPPORT AREA, 13th Bn. moving up to FRONT LINE. Battalion disposed as under :-	
			Batln Hqrs.} B.3.o.c. 'B' Coy SUBSIDIARY LINE 'D' Coy} 'C' ' ASYLUM. 'A' Coy in CELLARS, RUE DE LA CRECHE, ARMENTIERES.	
			Owing to expected attack at CHELUVELT at dawn tomorrow, all ranks slept in their gas helmets at the 'ALERT', fully aroused, and ready to move at once.	

Army Form C. 2118.

WAR DIARY
or
INTELLIGENCE SUMMARY.

(Erase heading not required.)

Instructions regarding War Diaries and Intelligence Summaries are contained in F. S. Regs., Part II. and the Staff Manual respectively. Title pages will be prepared in manuscript.

Place	Date	Hour	Summary of Events and Information	Remarks and references to Appendices
	July 28		Battalion in SUPPORT AREA. Working parties supplied as per working party table. 2 Patrols sent out on the 13th Bn.R.W.F. front.	

E. Gabb Kelly Lieut Col.
Commanding, 16th (S) Bn R.W.Fusiliers.

16th Bn. Royal Welsh Fusiliers

War Diary

For

March – 1918

Army Form C. 2118.

16th (S) R. Welsh Rgt.
113th Infantry Brigade
38th (Welsh) Division

WAR DIARY
or
INTELLIGENCE SUMMARY.
(Erase heading not required.)

MARCH 1918

Place	Date	Hour	Summary of Events and Information	Remarks and references to Appendices
	May 1/2		Battalion in SUPPORT AREA - ARMENTIERES SECTOR. Disposition as under:- Battn. Hqrs.} B.30.c. 'D' Coy } 'B' Coy SUBSIDIARY LINE 'C' Coy ASYLUM 'A' Coy in CELLARS, RUE DE LA CRECHE, ARMENTIERES. Supplied Working Parties as per Working Party Table.	
	2nd		Relieved in the SUPPORT AREA by the 13th Bn R.W.F. from FRONT LINE. Battalion moved to RESERVE BILLETS in ERQUINGHEM.	
	4/14th		'A' and 'D' Coys together with Special Platoons of 'B' and 'C' Coys. training for Special Enterprise. Digging REPLICA, rehearsals on REPLICA, both day and night, after training programme. Working Parties supplied by 'B' and 'C' Coys. Patrols sent out nightly to reconnoitre ground over which operation is to be carried out. REINFORCEMENTS - O.Rs - 6. 8/3/18 CASUALTIES - O.R - 1 WOUNDED - GAS. 13/3/18. OFFICERS - 2/Lt W.G. LLOYD - WOUNDED - 14/3/18.	

Army Form C. 2118.

WAR DIARY
or
INTELLIGENCE SUMMARY
(Erase heading not required.)

Place	Date	Hour	Summary of Events and Information	Remarks and references to Appendices
	May 15th		During the evening of the 15th, the two Companies, 'A' 'D' and special platoons of B.C. moved up to the assembly positions. Headquarters being established at trench line Bed W. and Advanced Hdqrs at Porte Egal.	
			At 10.7 p.m. under cover of Artillery, T.M. and M.G. barrage the raiding party together with School R.Es. entered enemy front and support lines. INCANDESCENT and SUPPORT TRENCHES. (I.11.a.) 15 Prisoners and 2 Light M.Gs. were captured, and at least 50 of the enemy reported to have been killed in the trenches and dugouts. 2 concrete dugouts and SUPPORT LINE were blown up.	
			In conjunction with this operation, a successful feint attack was made at the same time on CENTRAL and INANE TRENCHES. Under cover of Artillery and M.G. fire, dummy figures were manipulated in NO MAN'S LAND in front of our line C.29.1 and C.29.2. and many coloured lights fired. This feint undoubtedly drew the majority of the retaliation on this area, and later enemy bombed his own wire in this vicinity. Our casualties were:—	
			OFFICERS — 2/LT J. RICHARDS — KILLED. 2/LT J.M. JONES — WOUNDED.	
			O. Rs. — 10 KILLED; 3 DIED OF WOUNDS; 4 MISSING; 33 WOUNDED.	

Army Form C. 2118.

WAR DIARY
or
INTELLIGENCE SUMMARY
(Erase heading not required.)

Instructions regarding War Diaries and Intelligence Summaries are contained in F. S. Regs., Part II. and the Staff Manual respectively. Title Pages will be prepared in manuscript.

Place: 3.

Date	Hour	Summary of Events and Information	Remarks and references to Appendices
MAR 16th		Raiding Party spent the morning in rest and cleaning up. During the evening the Battn. relieved the 13th Bn. R.W.F. in the FRONT SECTOR — ARMENTIERES SECTOR. Relief complete 10.7 p.m.	
17th		Enemy activity slightly above normal. 11.45 a.m. 20 rounds 10.5 cm on SUBSDY. LINE I.9.c. 12.30 p.m.–12.50 p.m. 60 rds 77 mm and 10.5 cm I.3. central. Hostile aircraft very active, flying high over our lines. Enemy O.Bs. along the whole front. Our artillery carried out neutralizing fire on enemy battery positions. Our T.M.s active during afternoon and evening. M.Gs. fired 960 rds during the night. Four patrols sent out. One patrol lying in wait at I.6.c.55.05 to watch for enemy patrols approaching dummies, and finally to bring the dummies to our line.	
		CASUALTIES — 2/LT L.F. CLARKE, WOUNDED. 1 O.R. KILLED.	
18th	9.55/10.35 a.m.	70 rds 10.5 cm around I.9.d.40.90. and I.9.a.20.65. During the day enemy made a liberal use of East Mull sand at 7.15–7.45 p.m.	

Army Form C. 2118.

WAR DIARY
or
INTELLIGENCE SUMMARY
(Erase heading not required.)

Instructions regarding War Diaries and Intelligence Summaries are contained in F. S. Regs., Part II. and the Staff Manual respectively. Title Pages will be prepared in manuscript.

Place	Date	Hour	Summary of Events and Information	Remarks and references to Appendices
	Mar 18		Just a rapid burst of gas shells on LEFT FRONT and SUBSIDIARY LINE I.4.a.; these were mixed with H.E. During the day our artillery carried out retaliation fire.	
		8 pm	A deserter gave himself up to the garrison of No. 4 POST (I.11.a.) Our M.Gs. fired 6,000 rds on enemy C.Ts. etc. 3 patrols (fighting) sent out during the night.	
			CASUALTIES — 2/Lt. W.I. WILLIAMS — DIED OF WOUNDS.	
	19th		Enemy artillery fairly active during the day. Visibility bad.	
		10 p.m	480 4" Gas Bombs were fired by the 'N' section Special Coy R.E. 1,000 projectors were to have been fired in conjunction with above, but owing to unfavourable wind this was postponed until 11.10 pm. Our artillery barraged INCANDESCENT SUPPORT according fire for above. 2 fighting patrols out during the night.	
	20th		During day enemy artillery carried out scattered fire at irregular intervals. Between 6 – 6.30 pm gas shells on I.3.a. and d. Battalion relieved in the FRONT SECTOR by the 14th R.W.F. Relief complete 10.35 p.m.	

Army Form C. 2118.

WAR DIARY
or
INTELLIGENCE SUMMARY.
(Erase heading not required.)

Place	Date	Hour	Summary of Events and Information	Remarks and references to Appendices
	May 20th		On relief Battalion moved into RESERVE, disposition as under:— Battn Headqr. B.30.c.20.00. 'A' Coy BILLETS B.30.c.30.10. B. Coy LAUNDRIES H.5.a. D. " do 'C' " do	
	21/24		Owing to gas shelling on morning of 21st, 'A' Coy left BILLETS at B.30.c.30.10. and moved to LAUNDRIES H.5.a. Supplied working parties as per Working Party Table, and carried out training. REINFORCEMENTS — 76 O.Rs.	
	24th		Battalion moved into SUPPORT during the evening. Disposition as under:— Battn. Hqrs and 'B' Coy at ASYLUM. 'D' and 'C' Coys in CELLARS, SACRE COEUR. 'A' Coy — BRICKFIELDS. DECORATIONS:— MILITARY MEDAL to following:— 370042 Pte E.T. ROWLANDS. 54500 Pte T. CROSS. 304464 " T.L. JONES. 30284 " R. SIMMS. 31335 Cpl R. ROBERTS. 60155 Cpl R. COULTHURST 27179 " E.C. CONNOR 34058 L/C W.J. THOMAS	

Army Form C. 2118.

WAR DIARY
or
INTELLIGENCE SUMMARY

(Erase heading not required.)

Instructions regarding War Diaries and Intelligence Summaries are contained in F. S. Regs., Part II. and the Staff Manual respectively. Title Pages will be prepared in manuscript.

Place	Date	Hour	Summary of Events and Information	Remarks and references to Appendices
	Mar 25/26		Supplied Working parties as per Working Party Table. Carried out firing practice on range.	
			During night of 26th SUPPORT AREA was taken over by 13th WELSH REGT., and 17th Bn R.W.F., on relief. Companies moved to BILLETS in ERQUINGHEM.	
			CASUALTIES — 3 O.R. WOUNDED.	
	27th		Battn in RESERVE. The day spent in cleaning up, and inspections. During the evening relieved 14th WELSH REGIMENT in FRONT SECTOR — HOUPLINES.	
	28th		Owing to bad visibility there was very little activity during the day. During the night a minor enterprise was carried out by a party of volunteers from all four Companies — 1 Officer and 21 O.R. The party entered INCANDESCENT TRENCH. Only one of the enemy sentries was seen. Bombs were thrown at this man but it is thought he ran down communication trench, as no trace of him could be found on our party entering the trench.	
			CASUALTIES — 3 O.R. WOUNDED.	
	29th/30th		Visibility very bad, activity below normal. During evening of 30th the Battn was relieved by 16th Bn Royal Scots on relief Battn moved to BILLETS in PONT. DE NIEPPE.	

Army Form C. 2118.

WAR DIARY
or
INTELLIGENCE SUMMARY

(Erase heading not required.)

Instructions regarding War Diaries and Intelligence Summaries are contained in F. S. Regs., Part II. and the Staff Manual respectively. Title Pages will be prepared in manuscript.

Place	Date	Hour	Summary of Events and Information	Remarks and references to Appendices

	Mar 3/1/18		Battalion proceeded by march route from PONT DE NIEPPE to BILLETS in ARREWAGE AREA.
			
			DECORATIONS :- MILITARY CROSS TO -
			  T/Lt. (A/Capt) J. FAIRCLOUGH
			  T/2/Lt F.T. LINTON
			  T/2/Lt E.C. DEACON D.C.M.
			
			J.T. Dunkin Major,
			Commanding 16th (S) Bn.R.W.Fus.	

113th Inf.Bde.
38th Div.

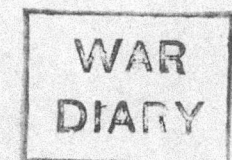

16th BATTN. THE ROYAL WELCH FUSILIERS.

A P R I L

1 9 1 8

16ᵗʰ Battalion R. W. Fus.

War Diary
April 1918

Army Form C. 2118.

WAR DIARY
or
INTELLIGENCE SUMMARY.

(Erase heading not required.)

16(S) Bn Royal Welsh Fusiliers
113th Infantry Brigade
38th (Welsh) Division

Instructions regarding War Diaries and Intelligence Summaries are contained in F. S. Regs., Part II. and the Staff Manual respectively. Title pages will be prepared in manuscript.

Place	Date	Hour	Summary of Events and Information	Remarks and references to Appendices
	1918 April 1st		Battalion marched from BILLETS in ARREWAGE to MERVILLE. Entrained at MERVILLE and proceeded by rail to MONDICOURT. Detrained at 8.45 p.m, and marched to BILLETS in HERISSART, arriving there about 4 am on the morning of the 2nd.	
	2nd		Morning spent in cleaning up. Battalion paraded at 1.30 p.m and marched to FORCEVILLE, ten on the line of march. Reinforcements – 63 Other Ranks.	
	3rd		Battalion paraded at 8.30 am and marched from BILLETS in FORCEVILLE to BILLETS in HERISSART. Owing to the large amount of traffic on the roads, progress was very slow, and frequent halts had to be made. Arrived HERISSART 11.30 a.m. Remainder of day spent in rest and cleaning up.	
	4th		Battalion should have taken part in Brigade scheme, but owing to rain, this was postponed. Training carried out in Billets, as far as possible.	
	5th		Carried out training during the morning. At 11.30 am received order to move. Battalion moved off, outfitting order, at 12.30 p.m. Preceded by fixed March to VADENCOURT. Embussed just outside the village. Battle Surplus sent back to HERISSART for this lacks and blankets, then proceeded to BILLETS in TOUTENCOURT.	

Army Form C. 2118.

WAR DIARY
or
INTELLIGENCE SUMMARY.
(Erase heading not required.)

Instructions regarding War Diaries and Intelligence Summaries are contained in F. S. Regs., Part II. and the Staff Manual respectively. Title pages will be prepared in manuscript.

Place	Date	Hour	Summary of Events and Information	Remarks and references to Appendices
	April 5th		Battalion remained in BIVOUACS for the night.	
	6th		During the evening the details from BILLETS at TOUTENCOURT, and the Battalion from BIVOUACS near VADENCOURT, proceeded to BILLETS at PIERREGOT.	
	7th		Day devoted to cleaning up etc.	
	8th		Battalion out on Brigade Scheme.	
	9th		Battalion out on Brigade Scheme.	
	10th		Battalion paraded 1.40 pm and proceeded by march route to BILLETS in HARPONVILLE, arriving at 5 pm.	
	11th		Day spent in cleaning up etc. During the afternoon, Battle Surplus and Transport Details proceeded to CONTAY. Battalion marched to the line during the evening and took over the BOUZINCOURT SECTOR, relieving the 6th Bn THE BUFFS. Disposition: 2 Companies in Front Line, 1 Company in Support, 1 in Reserve.	
	12th / 15th		Battalion holding line as above. With the exception of the morning of the 12th the line was fairly quiet. Our casualties were:— KILLED 3 O.R. WOUNDED 7 O.R. On the night of the 15th the Battn was relieved by the 14th Bn R. W. Kent and	

WAR DIARY or INTELLIGENCE SUMMARY

Army Form C. 2118.

Place	Date	Hour	Summary of Events and Information	Remarks and references to Appendices
	April 15th		Proceeded to BIVOUACS at BOUZINCOURT.	
			REINFORCEMENTS – 2/Lt W.C. HUGHES.	
	16th		In Bivouacs above Bouzincourt working parties as called for.	
	17th		Supplied working parties. During the evening two companies were relieved by two Coys of 10th S.W.B. Our two Coys proceeded to Billets in WARLOY.	
	18th		Remainder of Batt. relieved by 10th S.W.B, and proceeded to Bivouacs near SENLIS. BOUZINCOURT was shelled almost continuously during the time the Batt. was there.	
	19th		During the afternoon the Batt. proceeded to Billets in WARLOY.	
	20/21		Both days spent in training for special operations.	
	21st		On the night of the 21st marched to the line, carrying special equipment, and relieved the 17th Bn R.W.F. in front of BOUZINCOURT. DISPOSITION:– 2 Companies in Front Line, and 2 in Supporting line. Battalion assembled in exact dispositions for the attack, and remained in them throughout the day, without any movement. Enemy aircraft carry action, making two reconnaissances over the line. Instructions for the attack were:– 1st Objective, Right – C Coy. Left – B Coy. 2nd " A " " D "	

Army Form C. 2118.

WAR DIARY
or
INTELLIGENCE SUMMARY.
(Erase heading not required.)

Place	Date	Hour	Summary of Events and Information	Remarks and references to Appendices
	April 21st	7.30pm	Object of the attack – To secure the high ground held by the enemy. Barrage opened, and the Battalion advanced in good order. The enemy barrage descended at 7.34 p.m. Battalion was met by very heavy Machine Gun barrage, which cause heavy casualties all Officers in "A", "C", and "D" Companies became casualties immediately, and "B" Coy had one Officer wounded. Except on the left, we failed to attain the first objective, and it was found impossible to advance. This being so, Battalion dug in, and remained in this position until the night of the 25th, when it was relieved by 17th Bn Raif. 17th Bn Lancashire Fusiliers had taken over the extreme left of the line on the previous night. Battn went in with strength of 14 Officers and 450 O.Rs. and came out with 5 Officers and 225 O.Rs. Casualties – Officers – Killed 2/Lt J. Fenton M.C. ,, W. S. Goff M.C. ,, W. P. Williams ,, H. Bennet ,, S. E. Jenkens Missing 2/Lt A. O. Davis ,, A. Green Wounded 2/Lt A. B. Brodie Lieut C. Stewart M.C. Other Ranks Killed – 38 Died of wounds – 8. Missing – 20 Wounded – 159	
	25th			

WAR DIARY
or
INTELLIGENCE SUMMARY.

Army Form C. 2118.

Place	Date	Hour	Summary of Events and Information	Remarks and references to Appendices
	April 25th		On relief the Battn moved to bivouacs near HENENCOURT. Reinforcements – 21 other Ranks.	
	26th		Day spent in rest, and cleaning up	
	27th		Marched from bivouacs at 4.30 a.m. Breakfast on the line of march. Arrived Billets in HERISSART 10.15 a.m. Details and Battle Surplus from CONTAY rejoined Battn. Remainder of day spent in rest. Reinforcements – 102 other Ranks.	
	28/30		Training carried out as per programmes	

A.T. Tudie Major.
Commanding, 16th (S) Bn R.I. Fus.

16 RWF
Vol 30

WAR DIARY
FOR MONTH OF
MAY 1918
16 R.W.F.

Army Form C. 2118.

16th (S) Bn Royal Welsh Fusiliers
113th Infantry Brigade
38th (Welsh) Division

WAR DIARY
or
INTELLIGENCE SUMMARY
(Erase heading not required.)

MAY 1918

Instructions regarding War Diaries and Intelligence Summaries are contained in F.S. Regs., Part II. and the Staff Manual respectively. Title pages will be prepared in manuscript.

Place	Date	Hour	Summary of Events and Information	Remarks and references to Appendices
	1918 MAY 1st		The Battalion (in Battle Order) marched from BILLETS in HERISSART to BIVOUACS at P.34.c.3.2, arriving at 12.10pm and relieved the 17th Bn Royal Scots. Parade at 7.30pm and proceeded to the line, and relieved 15th Bn Cheshire Regt, in the Right Bn Front, Centre Bde, Sector, AVELUY SECTOR. Relief complete 12.30am.	
	2nd		Enemy fired intermittently on C.T.s and W.8.D and W.9.a by day, in bursts by night up to 9.30pm, BOUZINCOURT shelled at intervals during the day. Flight of E.A's over our lines at 4 pm, heavily engaged by R.A. and L.G. fire. Our artillery active during the day on back areas. 18 fires and 45 hits fired on Road W.18.a and b. Direct hits on transport large amount of hostile movement noticed on AVELUY ROAD W.18.A+B. Suspected relief in progress, artillery informed. Patrol out from 9.30pm to midnight.	
			Casualties:- 1 O.R. wounded.	
			Reinforcements:- Officers:- Capt. J.M.W. Barker. 2/Lt A.H. Harris " Eric Eccles " V.E. Maley	

WAR DIARY
or
INTELLIGENCE SUMMARY.

(Erase heading not required.)

Army Form C. 2118.

Place	Date	Hour	Summary of Events and Information	Remarks and references to Appendices
	3rd		Activity above normal all day. Visibility good, aircraft busy patrolling the line all day. During the night Battn extended its RIGHT Boundary to conform to new Bde Bndy, taking over extra front from 10th S.W.B. Fighting Patrol out from 9.30pm to midnight.	
	4th		Enemy artillery not quite so active as yesterday. Aircraft – above normal. Our artillery quiet during the morning, but very active during the afternoon and night. Our aircraft showed great activity. At 7.0 pm 50 to 60 planes patrolled behind our lines in a Northerly direction. Large formations over enemy line at 9-10 pm. Movement on Road in W.18.A and B engaged by our artillery and good results obtained. Northern Boundary of Battn Known area was adjusted at midnight to W.8 A 95.90. Fighting patrol out from 9.30pm — 12.30 am. Reinforcements. – 159 Other Ranks.	
	5th		Activity normal during the day. During the night the Battn was relieved by the 13th Bn R.W.F., and on relief moved to Bivouacs at V.5.A. Casualties:- 2 Other Ranks KILLED	

WAR DIARY

3.

PLACE	DATE	HOUR	SUMMARY OF EVENTS AND INFORMATION.
	6th		Morning spent in cleaning up. At noon 'A' Coy took up position in the BOUZINCOURT — ENGLEBELMER LINE as garrison.
			Casualties — 1 OR. wounded.
			Reinforcements — Officers — Lieut J. Molyn
			2/Lt L. Williams
			" C. Pickering
			" WmCown
			" A. Tatt
	7th 8th 9th		Battalion in RESERVE as above. Company in the BOUZINCOURT — ENGLEBELMER LINE changed daily. Supplied working parties as per table.
			Casualties — Officers — 2/Lt R.W. Thomas — KILLED (attd T.M.B)
			1 OR. wounded (attd T.M.B).
			Decorations — MILITARY MEDAL to :-
			18327 Cpl. C. Daniels. 34555 Pte J.C. White.
			54453 Pte J. Tearnett 6678 " H. Jones
			19538 Cpl. J.C. Arnott 20948 " J.G. Jones.
			19135 Sgt G. Lloyd.
			During the night of the 9/10th the Battn. relieved the 14th Bn. R.W.F. in LEFT Battn. Front, CENTRE SECTION, AVELUY SECTOR. Relief complete 11.25 pm.

WAR DIARY

PLACE	DATE	HOUR	SUMMARY OF EVENTS AND INFORMATION.
	10th	9 p.m.	ZERO HOUR – In accordance with operation orders, 114th Inf. Bde on our LEFT carried out an attack with the object of capturing and holding a line running from the South West corner of AVELUY WOOD (W.10 a. 80 96) to the note at W.4.c. 80.00 and thence to present front line at W.4.t. 30.60. Battn. to be prepared to join up with 114th Bde in event of attack proving successful. As the objective was not gained, no movement took place on part of Battn. Our aircraft very active during operation. In addition to fire during attack, our artillery kept up harassing fire during day & night. Fighting patrol out from 10.30 p.m. – midnight. CASUALTIES. – 1 O.R. WOUNDED.
	11th		Enemy artillery quiet during the day with exception of "crashes" on BOUZINCOURT. Our artillery active during day, and carried out harassing fire according to programme at night. Owing to poor visibility, aerial activity below normal.

WAR DIARY.

PLACE	DATE	HOUR	SUMMARY OF EVENTS AND INFORMATION
	11th		Fighting patrol out from midnight to 2.30 am Casualties - 1 OR killed (attd Surveying Co).
	12th		Enemy artillery fairly quiet during day with exception of usual "Crumps" on BOUZINCOURT. Slight activity along whole front line during the night, both artillery and M.G. Our artillery active day and night, according to programme. Our planes very active in the evening and night. Enemy used many searchlights from AVELUY WOOD. Fighting Patrol out from midnight to 2.30 am
	13th		Activity below normal all day owing to poor visibility. A fighting patrol of 1 Officer, 10 Riflemen, and a Lewis Gun Team left our line at W.9.a 72.28 at 11 pm with object of capturing m.g. at W.9.d. 60 32. This was unsuccessful owing to the presence of enemy wire. Lewis Company relief - complete 11.45 p.m. Reinforcements - Officers 2/Lt T.W.Holland
	14th		Enemy artillery activity normal. 1.30 p.m. Hostile plane attacked our O.B. WEST of BOUZINCOURT and set it on fire. Our aircraft very active, and one formation brought down the E.A. which fired our O.B.

WAR DIARY.

PLACE	DATE	HOUR	SUMMARY OF EVENTS AND INFORMATION
AVELUY WOOD	May 14th		Our planes very active during the night. Many searchlights used from AVELUY WOOD. Fighting patrol out from 11 pm to 1 am.
	15th		Artillery very active on both sides during the day, visibility good. 15 cm Hows registered on BOUZINCOURT during afternoon. Our aircraft patrolling enemy front from 7.0 am onwards at low altitudes. Reconnoitring patrol of 1 NCO and 4 men out from 10.30 pm to 12.30 am. Casualties — 2 ORs wounded
	16th		Enemy artillery very active. Direct hit on Church Tower MARTINSART, destroying it. Enemy snipers very active from AVELUY WOOD. Our artillery carried out shoots according to programme and fired on movement, aircraft also very active. Enemy plane dropped 6 bombs near Reserve Line W.&.a. and 4 at 1.0 am. Reconnoitring patrol of 1 Officer and 4 ORs left our lines at 11.30 pm and returned 1.30 am. Inter-Company relief carried out. Casualties — 1 OR wounded.

WAR DIARY.

PLACE	DATE	HOUR	SUMMARY OF EVENTS AND INFORMATION.
	MAY 17th	10.0 am - 1 pm	Our artillery carried out special shoot and again from 6pm - 7pm. No enemy retaliation except for four 15 cm on our W.Z.B. about 11 am. Very few E.A's seen, a few very high over enemy line. Our aircraft very active. One of our reconnoitring patrols approached within 10 yards of enemy post at W.9.B.60.40 where Stick bombs were thrown at them causing two casualties.

Casualties - 2 O.Rs killed, 7 O.Rs wounded.
Decorations - 2/Lt I.B. Price   M.C.
                    " W. Young M.C.

15478 C.S.M. Norton W.   D.C.M.
19091 Cpl.   Chadwick I.R. D.C.M.
36989 "   Newport A.   D.C.M. |
| | 18th | | Artillery on both sides very active throughout the day. Our artillery carried out special shoot between 10 am and 1 pm. In conjunction with 13th Welsh Regt on our left and 14th Welsh on our right the Bat carried out a raid on M.G. post at W.9.t.60.30. Artillery and T.M. co-operation as per programme. ZERO hour 10.30 pm. Enemy retaliated with heavy barrage on Support Line, and large quantities |

WAR DIARY

PLACE	DATE	HOUR	SUMMARY OF EVENTS AND INFORMATION
	18th		H 20 shells on battery positions in valley W.1.A and V.6.D. Nailing party found enemy posts unoccupied. Our aircraft very active all day.
			Casualties - Officers - Lieut J.M.W Barker - Wounded
			O.Rs - 3 Killed
			1 Died of wounds.
			5 Wounded.
	19th		Aircraft and artillery active all day observation good. During the night 18/19 the Battn was relieved by the 18th Highland Light Infantry.
		10.30 p.m	enemy opened heavy bombardment of our front and rear areas. Our own artillery opened fire on SOS lines. On relief Battn proceeded to HARPONVILLE and remainder of night spent in field outside village.
			Casualties - O.Rs - 2 Killed
			5 Wounded
	20th		Reveille 6.30 a.m. Proceeded by march route to BILLETS in RUBEMPRE, arrived about 11.50 a.m. Remainder of day spent in rest and cleaning up.
			Casualties - O.Rs - 1 Wounded.
			Reinforcements - O.Rs - 3.

WAR DIARY.

PLACE	DATE	HOUR	SUMMARY OF EVENTS AND INFORMATION
	21/26		Battalion occupying Billets in RUBEMPRE. Carried out training. Training Grounds T.14.c.5.9.
			22/5/18 - Reinforcements 1 Officer - Capt. E.P. Andrews. 2/Lt G. Mack.
	27th		Battalion in Brigade Counter-attack scheme.
	28th		Battalion carried out Tank Exercise in conjunction with other units of Brigade, and "B" Coy 3rd Tank Battalion.
	29th		Carried out Training.
	30th		Morning spent in rehearsal for inspection by Corps Commander tomorrow. Shooting preliminary R.F.A. Competition in the afternoon.
	31st		Corps Commander inspected 113th Brigade Group on field at T.14.c.5.9. Remainder of day spent in training.

Stanwill
Lieut-Colonel,
Commanding. 16th (S) Bn. R.W.Fus'rs

16th BATT. ROYAL WELSH FUSILIERS.

WAR DIARY

FOR

JUNE 1918.

Vol 31

Army Form C. 2118.

16th (S) Bn R.W.F.
113th Infantry Bde.
38th (Welsh) Division.

WAR DIARY
or
INTELLIGENCE SUMMARY.
(Erase heading not required.)

JUNE 1918.

Place	Date	Hour	Summary of Events and Information	Remarks and references to Appendices
	1918 JUNE 1		Battalion occupying Billets in RUBEMPRE. Training carried out under Battn arrangements. Team from the Battn won the following prizes at the Bde. Rifle Meeting:- A.R.A. Competition. 2nd Prize (£14). 9 Platoon, C'Coy. Falling Plate Competition. 1st Prize (130 fcs) 14 Platoon 'D' Coy. Snapshooting " 1st Prize (80 fcs) 9 " 'B' " Lewis Gun " 1st Prize (£9) Decorations:- 54408. Pte F. JENKS. — BAR TO MILITARY MEDAL	
	2nd		Divine Service, and training carried out under Battn arrangements. Battn team - 14 Platoon D'Coy won the Falling Plate Competition at Divisional Rifle Meeting. REINFORCEMENTS: - 8. O.Rs.	
	3rd		Battle Surplus Personnel proceeded to 38th Div Reception Camp. Battalion carried out training on the manoeuvre area - patrols, and Raiding.	
	4th		Training as above. During the afternoon the Battn received through Bn Orders.	
	5th		Battalion Parade 9am. Proceeded by march route to bivouacs at FORCEVILLE	

Army Form C. 2118.

WAR DIARY
or
INTELLIGENCE SUMMARY.
(Erase heading not required.)

Place	Date	Hour	Summary of Events and Information	Remarks and references to Appendices
	1918. JUNE. 5th		Dinner on line of march. After the halt for dinner, the Transport Details fell in rear of Battn and proceeded to BILLETS in LEALVILLERS. One Company took up positions in SUPPORT LINE. ('C' Coy)	
	6th		Carried out training during the morning. Relieved the 14th R.W.F. in SUPPORT AREA during the night, commencing at 9 p.m. On completion of move, Battn was disposed as follows:- Left Front 'D' Coy, Right Front 'C' Coy, Left Support 'B' Coy, Right Support 'A' Coy. Battalion H.Q. in ENGLEBELNER, Q.19.&.65.10. REINFORCEMENTS — 4 O.Rs CASUALTIES — 1 O.R. WOUNDED.	

	7th 8th 9th 10th		Battn. employed on various working parties. CASUALTIES LT L WILLIAMS — WOUNDED 7/6/18
			                     1 O R — " "
			                      " — " 9th
			                      1 — " 10th
			
			DECORATIONS — KING'S BIRTHDAY HONOURS GAZETTE DATED 3RD JUNE, 1918
			D.S.O LIEUT. COLONEL E.J. DE P. O'KELLY.
			M.C HON CAPT. & Q.M. A.T. NEWELL	

WAR DIARY
OR
INTELLIGENCE SUMMARY

Army Form C. 2118.

Place	Date	Hour	Summary of Events and Information	Remarks and references to Appendices
	JUNE 10TH		D.C.M. 17705 L/CPL R.W. EVANS, ATTD T.M.B. MENTIONED IN DESPATCHES LIEUT. COL. E.J. de P. O'KELLY, D.S.O, CAPT. H.G. LEWIS, 2/LT E. THOMAS. 17822 C.S.M. F.E. WEBB. M.S.M. 18936 Sgt C ROOKS 19184 Sgt DODGSON J. Supplied work and wiring parties. Battn HQ moved to Q.23.a.9.3. (MAP - 57 D S.E.) CASUALTIES - 2 O.Rs. WOUNDED.	
	11th			
	12th		Companies employed on minor working parties during the day. Battn digging new trench on left of CHARLES AVENUE during the night. Heavy shelling round Battn HQ all day. CASUALTIES - 4 O.Rs. WOUNDED.	
	13th		Heavy Shelling near area occupied by H.Q., over 1,000 shells sent over during early morning, and 1 Officer and about 30 men were affected. During the night relieved the 13th R.W.F. in LEFT SUB-SECTION, MESNIL SECTOR. Relief Complete 11.40 p.m. Three Coys in front line and one in Support. Battn H.Q. Q.28.a.9.8.	

Army Form C. 2118.

WAR DIARY
or
INTELLIGENCE SUMMARY.
(Erase heading not required.)

Place	Date	Hour	Summary of Events and Information	Remarks and references to Appendices
	JUNE 14th		Activity below normal all day. Our artillery shelled ridge in Q.23.c and 23.d. at intervals during the day. Enemy our heavy shoot of all calibres on Q.29.t. from 5 to 6 p.m. From 7.30 p.m. our aircraft very active. Patrol sent out at midnight to reconnoitre enemy post at Q.23.c.95.25. CASUALTIES – 2 O.Rs. WOUNDED.	
	15th		Normal activity all day. Both artilleries fired intermittently during the day. Reconnoitring patrol left our lines at 1 a.m. to ascertain whether enemy holds a post at Q.23.d.05.42.	
	16th	6–7 a.m.	20 rds L.H.V. on CHARLES AVE., during the morning enemy Heavy Artillery shelled our back areas.	
		1.30–2 p.m.	20 L.T.Ms on CRAB TRENCH. Our howitzers shelled back areas during the day.	
		7.35 p.m.	35 and 18 pdrs on Q.11.t. and Q.12.d.	
		7.45 p.m.	36 of our 'planes crossed enemy line and engaged enemy 'planes. A fighting patrol left our lines at 11.30 p.m. to engage any hostile parties, and locate post near Q.23.d.05.40. CASUALTIES – 2 O.Rs. KILLED. 2 O.Rs. WOUNDED.	

WAR DIARY
or
INTELLIGENCE SUMMARY.
(Erase heading not required.)

Army Form C. 2118.

Place	Date	Hour	Summary of Events and Information	Remarks and references to Appendices
	JUNE 17th	6–7 am	80 rds 5.9 on our SUPPORT LINE.	
		7 am–1 pm	80 to 90 rds L.H.V. on Q.29.	
		7–8 am	30 rds 6" shell on Q.8. Our heavies fired on rear areas during the day.	
		9 pm – midnight	M.G. active.	
		10.45 pm	Fighting patrol left our lines at 10.45pm to reconnoitre enemy post at Q.23.d.05.40, with a view to "cut out" same.	
	18th	9.30 am	One of our planes flying low, was brought down by A.A. Gun fire. Enemy put four rounds on FRONT and SUPPORT LINES during the day. Our heavies shelled back areas at intervals. Our planes active over enemy lines all day.	
		9.45 pm	Fighting patrol left our lines with same object as last night.	
	19th	2 am – 3.20 am	Heavy bombardment of CRAB TRENCH. A few rounds on RIDGE TRENCH and HAMEL OUTPOSTS during the day. Our heavy hows. bombarded R.24–25 at 2 pm and 5 pm.	
		9.45 pm	Fighting patrol left our lines at Q.23.c.90.05 to engage any hostile patrols. In view of bombardment tomorrow all front system held as lightly as possible. Evacuated positions to be re-occupied at conclusion of operation.	

Army Form C. 2118.

WAR DIARY
or
INTELLIGENCE SUMMARY.
(Erase heading not required.)

Place	Date	Hour	Summary of Events and Information	Remarks and references to Appendices
	JUNE.			
	20th	2 am	Coys Artillery and MGs barraged enemy trenches and communications but no infantry action took place. Special Coy RE discharged smoke and gas.	
		2 - 3.20 am	enemy retaliated intermittent shelling on both sides during the day.	
		10 - 10.30 pm	Heavy bombardment of enemy lines.	
		3 - 5 pm	50 rds 6" Newtons on Q.23.	
			Fighting patrol proceeded to same front as previous nights (Q.23 d.05.40) Enemy aircraft very active during the evening.	
			CASUALTIES — 1 O.R. WOUNDED.	
	21st	2 am	14th and 2nd R.W.F. carried out raid on enemy trenches in front of MESNIL. Our front system was thinned in anticipation of enemy retaliation, which, however, was not very heavy. The above operation was covered by heavy artillery & M.G. barrage.	
		10.40 - 11 am	Three enemy planes patrolling our lines were driven back by two of our planes.	
		7 am - 8 am	15 rds 4.2 on BARN TRENCH. 10.30 - 11.30 am 30 rds 77mm on Q.28.	
		2.30 - 3.20 pm	a few shells on CRAB TRENCH and RIDGE SUPPORT.	

Army Form C. 2118.

WAR DIARY
or
INTELLIGENCE SUMMARY.
(Erase heading not required.)

Instructions regarding War Diaries and Intelligence Summaries are contained in F. S. Regs., Part II. and the Staff Manual respectively. Title pages will be prepared in manuscript.

Place	Date	Hour	Summary of Events and Information	Remarks and references to Appendices
	JUNE			
	21st	10.-11 pm	30 rds heavy H.E. on Q. 27. d.	
			Our artillery activity normal. Our M.G. very active during the night.	
		9 pm	Fighting patrol left our lines to lie in wait for enemy at Q.23.d.05.40	
			2 Reconnoitring parties sent out to clear NO MAN'S LAND of any dead	
			or wounded. CASUALTIES - 1 O.R. KILLED. 2 O.R. WOUNDED.	
	22nd		Usual artillery fire during the day	
			The Battalion was relieved during the night 22/23rd by the 17th R.W.F.	
			and on relief proceeded to camp at P.27.b.9.2. Battn HQ. in	
			FORCEVILLE. CASUALTIES - 1 O.R. KILLED. - 1 O.R. WOUNDED.	
	23rd	3.30 am	Relief complete. Battn in RESERVE, spent the day in cleaning up	
			and resting.	
			REINFORCEMENTS - 13 O.Rs	
	24th		Carried out Training during the day.	
		12 midnight	FORCEVILLE shelled by H.V. guns. Several shells near H.Qrs.	
			CASUALTIES - 1 O.R. WOUNDED.	
	25th 26th		2 Coys Training and 2 Coys on work at P.32.b.1.1 and BROWN LINE. - Construction of Defenced Order of Coys reversed on second day.	

Army Form C. 2118.

WAR DIARY
or
INTELLIGENCE SUMMARY.
(Erase heading not required.)

Place	Date	Hour	Summary of Events and Information	Remarks and references to Appendices
	JUNE 27th		Companies carried out training during the morning. Officers and N.C.Os. practice attack (without troops) on ACHEUX WOOD. During afternoon the whole Battn practice attack on ACHEUX WOOD.	
	28th		Lecture by Commanding Officer. Inspection of platoons by C.O. Demonstration of firing the No. 36 Grenade.	
		5 pm	Whole Battn working on PURPLE LINE. — Task completed about midnight.	
	29th		Recreational training during the morning. Training and Lectures in the afternoon.	
	30th		Morning spent on work and tactical exercises. Recreational Training during the afternoon.	

S/Aumothy
Lieut Colonel,
Commanding, 16th (S) Bn Royal Welsh Fus.

16TH BATT. ROYAL WELSH FUSILIERS
WAR DIARY
FOR
JULY 1918

Vol 32

D.S.

32 F
6 sheets

1.

WAR DIARY
or
INTELLIGENCE SUMMARY.
(Erase heading not required.)

Army Form C. 2118.

16th (S) Bn R.W.Fuslrs
113th Infantry Brigade
38th (Welsh) Division.

JULY, 1918.

Place	Date	Hour	Summary of Events and Information	Remarks and references to Appendices
	1918 July 1st		Battalion in Brigade Reserve at FORCEVILLE, P.27 & Q.2. Supplied Working Parties, and carried out training during the day. During the evening relieved the 19th Bn R.W.F., in the SUPPORT AREA, Batton Headquarters at Q.26.b.60.60. 1 Company of 14th R.W.F. attached to Battalion for work, etc. CASUALTIES - 1 O.R. WOUNDED.	
	2nd		Supplied Working Parties as per Brigade Table, and carried out Training.	
		9-11 p.m.	Enemy Gas shells on Q.26.b. and Q.20.d. Enemy bombarded the whole corps front. CASUALTIES - 1 O.R. WOUNDED.	
	3rd (4th)		Supplied Working Parties and carried out Training as above. Front line system reconnoitred. 3rd - CASUALTIES - 1 OFFICER WOUNDED - 2/Lt A.H.HARRIS. 1 O.R. KILLED 1 O.R. WOUNDED. REINFORCEMENTS - 2/Lt W.H.HARRIS.	

Army Form C. 2118.

WAR DIARY
or
INTELLIGENCE SUMMARY.
(Erase heading not required.)

Place	Date	Hour	Summary of Events and Information	Remarks and references to Appendices
	JULY 5th		Supplied Working Parties, and carried out Training. During the night relieved the 13th R.W.F. in the RIGHT FRONT SECTOR, MESNIL SECTOR. Battalion Headquarters at Q.28.a.95.40. Relief complete 12 midnight.	
	6th		Activity normal throughout the day. Hostile planes attempted to cross our lines during the day, but were driven back by M.G. and A.A. fire. Enemy M.G. very active during the night. Patrol sent out, but no enemy patrols encountered. Lt Col E J de P. O'Kelly, D.S.O, and 1 O.R. wounded whilst visiting our outpost line. Capt Fairclough M.C. assumed temporary command of the Battalion.

CASUALTIES — 1 OFFICER WOUNDED —
Lt.Col. E.J. de P. O'KELLY, D.S.O.
2 O.Rs. WOUNDED. | |
| | 7th | | Artillery activity all day. 11 am – 4 pm about 100 rds 4.2 on Q.34.F. and Q.28.d. Several rounds of 18 pdr fell short on BRECON and | |

WAR DIARY
or
INTELLIGENCE SUMMARY.
(Erase heading not required)

Army Form C. 2118.

Place	Date	Hour	Summary of Events and Information	Remarks and references to Appendices
BRACKEN TRENCHES	1918 JULY 7th		Some of these afterwards recovered and found to be marked 1915. Our 'planes very active. 3 Patrols out on the Battalion front, and body of 2nd R.W.F. man brought in. CASUALTIES = 3 ORs KILLED, 2 " WOUNDED.	
	8th	1.30 a.m.	Enemy party of about 12 men attempted to raid 'F' POST, Q.35.a.70.35. but were driven off by bombing. A search was at once made, but no identifications secured. Normal activity during the day.	
		10 p.m.	Enemy lines heavily bombarded with all calibres.	
		11.30 p.m.	6 6" shells fell short on Q.34.a. Our M.Gs. and L.Gs. very active during the night. CASUALTIES = 2 O.Rs. WOUNDED.	
	9th		Activity normal during the day. On the night 9th/10th the Batt'n was relieved by the 10th Bn S.W.B. Major E. HELME, 15th Bn WELSH REGT., assumed temporary command of the Battalion.	

Army Form C. 2118.

WAR DIARY
or
INTELLIGENCE SUMMARY.
(Erase heading not required.)

Instructions regarding War Diaries and Intelligence Summaries are contained in F. S. Regs., Part II. and the Staff Manual respectively. Title pages will be prepared in manuscript.

Place	Date	Hour	Summary of Events and Information	Remarks and references to Appendices
	JULY 10th		On relief Battalion moved to RESERVE AREA, FORCEVILLE, P.21.d. Battalion Headquarters at P.21.d.4.7. Relief complete 5.30.a.m. Morning devoted to rest and cleaning up. Training carried out during the afternoon.	
	11th to 18th		Supplied Working Parties and carried out training daily.	
	18th		LT. COL. C.E. DAVIES assumed Command of the Battalion. MAJOR E HELME rejoined 15TH WELSH REGT. REINFORCEMENTS — 2/Lt W. OWEN. 16 O.R.s.	
	19th		Battalion Parade 3.50 a.m., moved off at 4.5 a.m. Proceeded by march route to new area in Corps Reserve at V.8.b. Breakfast on arrival. The morning devoted to rest. Cleaning up and training during the afternoon.	
	20th 22	8.45 pm	Supplied Working Parties and carried out training. On receiving 'Alarm' order Battalion took battle	

Army Form C. 2118.

WAR DIARY
or
INTELLIGENCE SUMMARY.
(Erase heading not required.)

Instructions regarding War Diaries and Intelligence Summaries are contained in F. S. Regs. Part II. and the Staff Manual respectively. Title pages will be prepared in manuscript.

Place	Date	Hour	Summary of Events and Information	Remarks and references to Appendices
	JULY 22nd		Surplus, proceeded to man BROWN LINE, in accordance with previous orders. Companies returned to camp independently on completion of operation. (Battn. Gardens). Sports held in the afternoon on Batn. Training ground V. 8. B.	
	23rd to 29th		Supplied Working Parties and carried out training. REINFORCEMENTS 23rd — OFFICERS 2/Lt. L. Saunders, 2/Lt. L. O. Owen, 2/Lt. G. E. Young, 2/Lt. E. J. Owen. 25th — O. Rs. — 21.	
	30th		Morning spent in clearing the camp, striking tents and bivouacs. Battalion Parade 12.45pm and moved off at 1pm. Proceeded by march route to BILLETS in ARQUEVES, arriving at 4pm.	
	31st		Battalion engaged on Outpost Scheme during the morning. Training carried out in the afternoon.	

C.D. Davis Lt.Col.
Commanding 16th (S) Bn R.W. Fus.

16th Batt Royal Welsh Fusiliers

WAR DIARY

FOR

AUGUST 1918

Army Form C. 2118.

WAR DIARY
or
INTELLIGENCE SUMMARY.

16th (S) Battn. R.W.Fus.
113th Infantry Brigade,
38th (Welch) Division

AUGUST 1918

Place	Date	Hour	Summary of Events and Information	Remarks and references to Appendices
	Aug 1st to 3rd		Battalion in training at ARQUEVES.	
	4th to 5th		Proceeded by march route to HERISSART. Training at HERISSART. Reinforcements - 2 O.Rs.	
	6th		Battalion paraded 8.55 a.m. and proceeded by march route to staging area near FORCEVILLE. During the night relieved the 12th Manchester Regt. in SUPPORT AREA, AVELUY LEFT SECTOR.	
	7th to 12th		Holding line as above. Casualties - 9 O.Rs. Wounded 8th. 2 O.Rs. 10th. On the night 12/13th the Battalion was relieved by the 14th R.W.F. On relief moved to Billets in FORCEVILLE, but later proceeded by march route to camp at TOUTENCOURT.	
	13th to 20th		Battalion carried out training in above area. Reinforcements 19 O.Rs.	
	21st		On the night 20/21st marched to Bivouac area at ENGINEER VALLEY, V.8.b. Carried out training in above area.	
	22nd		Battalion moved from ENGINEER VALLEY, to V.24.b. area NORTH of MILLENCOURT, where it bivouaced at 9am for day. March up to V.26. area	

WAR DIARY
or
INTELLIGENCE SUMMARY.
(Erase heading not required.)

Army Form C. 2118.

Place	Date	Hour	Summary of Events and Information	Remarks and references to Appendices
	Aug 22nd		West of ALBERT and bivouaced for night. Casualties - 1 O.R. Wounded.	
	23rd		Day spent in last night's area, completing equipment, and issuing operation orders. Battalion moves forward to assembly positions at 9 p.m. All in position with 14th R.W.F. on Left and 18th Div. on Right by 12 midnight.	
	24th		Barrage opened 1.0 am and attack progressed well. 'B' Coy captured 1st Objective - LA BOISELLE. 'A', 'C', & 'D' Coys passed 2nd Objective and took up position about X.14.b. and d. Considerable trouble was experienced after daybreak by concealed enemy machine guns and snipers behind our new line. Casualties - Officers Lieut. J. MOSTYN W.D. at Duty 2/Lt H.J. OWEN Killed. O.Rs. 11 Killed 46 Wounded. At 4.30 pm Battalion moved off in pursuit of enemy. 16th R.W.F. on Right, 14th R.W.F. on Left, and 13th R.W.F in Reserve. The advance was continued with little opposition to Western outskirts of CONTALMAISON where we were held up by enemy M.Gs. and T.M.	
	25th		At 2.30 am Battn attacked CONTALMAISON under Artillery barrage. Attack successful. Objective gained and Coys in position by 5 a.m.	

WAR DIARY
or
INTELLIGENCE SUMMARY.
(Erase heading not required.)

Army Form C. 2118.

Place	Date	Hour	Summary of Events and Information	Remarks and references to Appendices
	Aug. 25th		Day spent in Outpost position from PEAKE WOOD to CEMETERY. H.Q. in CHATEAU CONTALMAISON. Casualties – Officers NIL O.Rs. 1 Killed 10 Wᵈ Coys concentrated on Western edge of MAMETZ WOOD at 5 p.m and prepare for attack towards LONGUEVAL. 'C' Coy push out patrols through wood and after overcoming opposition occupied Eastern edge of WOOD.	
	26th		At 4 am Brigade attack towards LONGUEVAL, 13th R.W.F. in front to take 1st Objective, 16th and 14th R.W.F. in rear on RIGHT and LEFT respectively, 2nd R.W.F. in rear as moppers-up. Battalion formed up at 3.30 am and rally East of MAMETZ WOOD and advanced under Artillery barrage. 13th R.W.F. captured 1st Objᵉ but 16th R.W.F. and 14th R.W.F. were held up by heavy M.G. fire from RIGHT flank, CATERPILLAR WOOD and MONTAUBAN. Line held during day approximately S.15.d.50.00 to S.15.d.50.00. 18th Div. attacked RIGHT flank at 9.30 a.m. Patrols of 6th DRAGOON GDS. ordered to clear village of LONGUEVAL but met with strong opposition and many casualties. Enemy still holding LONGUEVAL and DELVILLE WOOD at night.	

WAR DIARY
or
INTELLIGENCE SUMMARY.
(Erase heading not required.)

Army Form C. 2118.

Place	Date	Hour	Summary of Events and Information	Remarks and references to Appendices
	Aug. 26th		Battn which had become very scattered was reformed at SABOT COPSE for night. Casualties — Capt. G. L. Andrew Killed 2/Lt W. H. Harris " 2/Lt W. Owen Died of wounds 2/Lt W. A. Paine wounded Capt. J. E. G. Halsey " 2/Lt G. D. T. Owen " 2/Lt T. S. Williams " O.Rs. 17 killed, 55 wounded, 1 missing	
	27th		Brigade in readiness for enemy counter-attack at 4. a.m. Brigade moves off at 9 and to attack LONGUEVAL and GINCHY without artillery support. 13th R.W.F. as Advance Guard. 16th & 14th R.W.F. in Rear on Right and left respectively. 13th R.W.F. held up by enemy M.Gs. in LONGUEVAL. 16th R.W.F. reached line of Road S. 17. c and d. and cleared some enemy nests. D Coy led by 2/Lt T. GEORGE advanced under cover of Rifle Grenade sections and repulsed enemy counter-attack on the left flank of the Battalion. Brigade withdrawn at 6 pm to WEST of LONGUEVAL to hill artillery bombarded village and MGs in WOOD. Moved later in night to BRENTIN-LE-GRAND as by T. GEORGE killed. Casualties — 2/Lt T. GEORGE killed. 6 ORs killed, 23 wounded.	

Army Form C. 2118.

WAR DIARY
or
INTELLIGENCE SUMMARY.
(Erase heading not required.)

Instructions regarding War Diaries and Intelligence Summaries are contained in F. S. Regs., Part II. and the Staff Manual respectively. Title pages will be prepared in manuscript.

Place	Date	Hour	Summary of Events and Information	Remarks and references to Appendices
	Aug 28th		Day spent in BAZENTIN-LE-GRAND area. At 4pm 'B' Coy ordered to push out patrols to Eastern edge of LONGUEVAL and hold village. Village reported clear at 6.30pm, and all other Coys moved up to WEST of village. 14th R.W.F. on LEFT, 13th R.W.F. in SUPPORT. Casualties 1 O.R. Wounded.	
	29th		Battalion attacked at 5.30 am under artillery barrage with 14th R.W.F. on LEFT and 13th R.W.F. in SUPPORT. Objective – GINCHY. Attack successful and line taken up 1000 yds EAST of village on high ground overlooking MORVAL. Little opposition and few casualties. Day spent improving line occupied. At 6pm attack started towards MORVAL with Artillery barrage 'A' Coy leading we held up by strong enemy position with numerous M.Gs in valley S.W. of MORVAL. Line eventually taken up along sunken road and RAILWAY by 'A' + 'B' Coys with 'D' Coy in CHALK PIT and 'C' Coy in RESERVE. Casualties – 2/Lt M. WADDINGTON WOUNDED O.Rs. 1 killed 5 wounded. Reinforcements – Officers – 2/Lt M. Waddington 2/Lt J. Richards	

Army Form C. 2118.

WAR DIARY
or
INTELLIGENCE SUMMARY.
(Erase heading not required.)

Place	Date	Hour	Summary of Events and Information	Remarks and references to Appendices
	Aug 30th		Day spent in positions taken up on night 29th, enemy shelled our foremost positions and H.Q. heavily at intervals during day. Brigade relieved by 114th Bde and withdrawn to cwm near SUGAR REFINERY in evening. Battn relieved by 15th Welch Regt at 8 pm. Casualties – 5 O.R. Killed, 31 wounded.	
	31st		Day spent in Reserve, refitting and reorganizing.	

O. Davis
Lieut. Col.
Commanding, 16th (S) Bn R.W. Fus.

WAR DIARY.
for September 1918.
16th Batt. ROYAL WELSH FUSILIERS.

WAR DIARY or INTELLIGENCE SUMMARY.

Army Form C. 2118.

(Erase heading not required.)

SEPTEMBER 1918

Place	Date	Hour	Summary of Events and Information	Remarks and references to Appendices
	Sept 1st		Enemy O.H. from SUGAR REFINERY at 2.15 a.m. & assembly positions South of LES BOEUFS in close support to 114th Bdn. who attacked. Mutual enemy Artillery barrage at 4 & 5.10 a.m. 113th Bdn. relieved the 114th Bdn. On their objective at 9.15 a.m. 16th Bn. RWF relieving 15th Welsh Regt. "B" Coy reached our position in front of village and captured about 30 prisoners. 50 prisoners were being mopped up in the village by other Coys.	
		5.30 p.m.	Attack on SAILLY SAILLISEL under Artillery barrage, 13th RWF on left, 14th RWF in reserve. Attack successful and objective gained by 9.30 p.m., about 50 prisoners captured by "D" Coy.	
			Casualties :- O.Rs. 4 killed. 2 wounded.	
	Sept 2nd		Day spent in outpost line East of SAILLY SAILLISEL. At 5 p.m. enemy Artillery barrage 115th Bdn. passed through to attack MESNIL-EN-ARROUAISE. Attack held up by M.Gs. Leaving 16th RWF still in front line. Enemy attempted counter attack on left division and brigade redistributed to meet this at night.	
			Casualties :- O.Rs. 2 killed. 17 wounded. 1 missing.	

Army Form C. 2118.

WAR DIARY
or
INTELLIGENCE SUMMARY.
(Erase heading not required.)

Instructions regarding War Diaries and Intelligence Summaries are contained in F. S. Regs., Part II. and the Staff Manual respectively. Title pages will be prepared in manuscript.

Place	Date	Hour	Summary of Events and Information	Remarks and references to Appendices
	Sept 3rd		Morning spent in line East of SAILLY SAILLISEL. 115th Bde. advanced to MESNIL-EN-ARROUAISE and reported some clear of the enemy. 113th Bde. followed in support at 2pm. 16th RWF in support to 13th & 14th RWF. Line taken up by 6pm in trenches West of village and Bn. Hqrs in LOON COPSE. Casualties:- ORs 3 killed 10 wounded.	
	Sept 4th		Day spent in line West of MESNIL - very little hostile artillery. Battalion under orders to cross TORTILLE RIVER in support of 114th Bde. Casualties:- Nil.	
	Sept 5th		Day spent in yesterday's positions. Little hostile activity. Relieved by 9th Bn. KOYLI at 5pm, and proceeded by march route to DELVILLE WOOD AREA arriving 10.30 pm.	
	Sept 6/9		Bn. in DELVILLE WOOD AREA. Reinforcement:- 76 ORs.	
	Sept 10		Battalion proceeded by march route to LE MESNIL EN ARROUAISE and spent night there.	
	Sept 11		Bn. proceeded at 5.30 pm and was relieved 6 line relieving the 10th Bn. Cheshires	

Army Form C. 2118.

WAR DIARY
or
INTELLIGENCE SUMMARY.
(Erase heading not required.)

Instructions regarding War Diaries and Intelligence Summaries are contained in F.S. Regs., Part II. and the Staff Manual respectively. Title pages will be prepared in manuscript.

Place	Date	Hour	Summary of Events and Information	Remarks and references to Appendices
	13th Sept to 16th Sept		Forester in Support Area, Rgt. Sectn in Engr Spare Q.32 area. Bn. Hdqrs at Q.32.d.3.4 (Ry Sqrs 57C SW 1/20,000 & 57C SE 1/20,000) Res Hdqrs remained in LE MESNIL EN ARROUAISE Area. Battalion in Support, LEFT SECTOR. Engr Spare Q.32. Specialist training carried out as far as circumstances permitted and carrying parties supplied. Casualties: OR 5 wounded.	
	16/17 Sept		113th Inf Bn. relieved 115th Inf Bn. in front line — 16th RWF in support and remaining in Q.32. a.m. Bn. Hdqrs moved to dugout at Q.32.a.3.5	
	17th Sept		Battalion env. Hdqrs in above area.	
	17/18 Sept		Battalion moved from Q.32 area at 2 a.m. to assembly positions for the attack in conjunction with 114th Inf. Bn. on the right and 5th Division on left. (2nd Bn. KOSB). Companies disposed as follows: — D Coy on R Right, 2 platoons A Coy in Centre, C Coy on R Left, 1 platoon A Coy in Support covering frontage of 2 leading platoons. B Coy in Reserve. Sector Boundaries: — D Coy from junction of trench and road at Q.36.c.30.50 to junction of trench and road Q.30.c.30.25 (inclusive)	

WAR DIARY
or
INTELLIGENCE SUMMARY.
(Erase heading not required.) (A)

Army Form C. 2118.

Place	Date	Hour	Summary of Events and Information	Remarks and references to Appendices
			C.Coy. Junction of Trench and Road Q.30.c.30.25. (inclusive) to Q.30.c.45.65. (2 platoons A Coy. covering frontage of 160* between C & D Coys) B. Coy. remain in AFRICAN TRENCH. A. Coy. furnished 1 platoon to CHURCH and 5th Division on its left, and D. Coy. furnished 1 platoon to liaison with Bn. on its right. 2 platoons 19th Bn. Welsh Regiment attached to each of leading companies, moving in rear of each wave, and employed in making L.G. nests. At 5.20 am Battalion attacked AFRICAN TRENCH under Artillery barrage. The trench was entered but C & D Coys were held up by enemy M.G. fire. D Coy was then ordered to send bombing party to Lion Trench and B Coy to reach Bn and meet D Coy. B Coy intended Saps E of AFRICAN TRENCH at Q.35.a.80.90. but was enfiladed by enemy M.Gs. from Q.35.a.95.20, Q.36.a.30.65 and Q.29.d.9.4. Batt. Left to waterman to AFRICAN SUPPORT. At 3.40 p.m 3 patrols were pushed forward to AFRICAN TRENCH to try and link up with 14th Bn RWF, but which was found to be held by	

WAR DIARY
or
INTELLIGENCE SUMMARY.

(Erase heading not required.)

Army Form C. 2118.

Place	Date	Hour	Summary of Events and Information	Remarks and references to Appendices
			To enemy in strength from Q.25.c.8.9 to Q.26.c.5.5 HQ.	
			Bn now occupied AFRICAN SUPPORT, and was in touch with 8th Division on left, and 14th Bn Butts on right.	
			The Batt was relieved after dark by the 13th RWF and 15th FRONT Bn, and moved to positions occupied by 13th Battn in D.1.d. North cutting E & W great river at Q.3.d.a.5.0 - move completed about 9 p.m.	
			Casualties during operations:-	
			Missing (Believed Killed) 2/Lt T.W. HOLLAND, 2/Lt J. RICHARDS.	
			2/Lt G.E. SAUNDERS, 2/Lt V.E. YOUNG	
			Wounded "	
			Capt I. GRIFFITH, Lt. V.R. HUGHES	
			Lt. S.G. YOUNG, 2/Lt. C. MACK. M.M.	
			2/Lt T.B. PRICE, M.C. 2/Lt D.E. LEWIS	
			2/Lt B. THOMAS	
			O.R's. Killed 13, Wounded 68, Missing (Believed Killed) 29.	
	19th Sept		B. Coy. returned to garrison AFRICAN SUPPORT within the limits of 14th RWF from C.T. in Q.35.a.2.6. to take over the SUPPORT line of the 14th RWF after the latter had attacked AFRICAN TRENCH. The Coy. was in touch with 14th RWF on the left and 13th Bn RWF on the right.	

WAR DIARY
or
INTELLIGENCE SUMMARY.

(Erase heading not required.)

Army Form C. 2118.

Instructions regarding War Diaries and Intelligence Summaries are contained in F. S. Regs., Part II. and the Staff Manual respectively. Title pages will be prepared in manuscript.

Place	Date	Hour	Summary of Events and Information	Remarks and references to Appendices
	20th Sep		14th Bn. RWF reported to have captured AFRICAN TRENCH, and C. Coy moved to position to reinforce 14th Bn. RWF. "C" Coy held line in AFRICAN TRENCH from Bn. Southern Boundary at Q.35.C.90.80 along to C.T. at Q.35.C.90.95" exclusive. "C" Coy relieved in AFRICAN TRENCH by 10th Bn SWB, and B. Coy relieved in AFRICAN SUPPORT by A Coy 2nd Bn RWF. On completion of relief both Coys. moved to trenches in Q.32. not occupied by 14th RWF. A and D Coys. (Reserve) relieved by 14th Bn. RWF and moved to trenches in Q.31. Bn Hqrs. moved to Q.32.A.2.4.	
	22nd Sep		At 12.30 p.m. Bn. moved by march route to 16. MESNIL EN ARROUAISE area, and remained in this area until 28th Sept.	
	26th Sep		Each day spent in cleaning up, checking stores, equipment, etc. Training and Range Firing carried out	
			Reinforcements:- 111 ORs	
			Major. S.L. MUNKIN. DSO to England to exchange	
			Major F.R.DALE joined Battn on 2nd in Command.	
	24th Sep		Officer Reinforcements:- 2/Lt. D.W.HOW 2/Lt. A.L.BURNS Lt. T. E.EVANS, MC } ORs - 7 2/Lt. T.B.KENNAN 2/Lt. J.M.DAVIES Lt. R.C.R. SHOPLAND} 2/Lt. G.W. CARR 2/Lt. F THOMPSON	

Army Form C. 2118.

WAR DIARY
or
INTELLIGENCE SUMMARY.
(Erase heading not required.)

Place	Date	Hour	Summary of Events and Information	Remarks and references to Appendices
	Sept 28th		Battn. proceeded 4.9a.m. and progressed by busses to HENDICOURT, and from W/S position in trenches EAST of village in W.22. Area. Rear Hdqrs established S.M SOREL-LE-GRAND	
	Sept 29th		1 Battn. in position occupied on night of 28th	
	Sept 30th		Reinforcements:- 2/Lt. R. PALFREYMAN. 13. O.R's. Casualties:- Nil.	

Awards during month :-

D.S.O.
Lt. Col. C.E. DAVIES.

M.C.
Cpl. R.E. WILLIAMS.
Cpl. W.A. PAINE.
2/Lt. O.M. WILLIAMS.
Major A.R. DBRE.

M.M. (Confirming)
18512 H/C. C. HYDE   6075 Sgt. J. MACEY   19179 Sgt. C. ANDREWS
43682 H/C. J. HUGHES   19911 Sgt. G.W. WHITTINGHAM   18067
61065 Pte. R. THOMAS   18845 Cpl. R. SHAW   40809 H/C. T. PARRY
53454 " D. EVANS   31662 Pte. G. HADFIELD
                         23530 H/C. E. HOWELLS.

Bar to M.M
568413 Cpl. R. WILLIAMS, M.M.,   19377 Cpl. R. ROBERTS, M.M.

D.C.M.
7892 C/R.S.M. R. ROHRER
58286 Pte. F. JONES.

M.M.
350015 Pte. C. MURPHY
21762 A/C.S.M. T. HAYTER
554444 Sgt. G.M. SLAUGHTER
23400 H/C. J. DODD
18434 C.S.M. C. WYNNE
235156 Pte. A. WATSON.
18067 Sgt. C.L. PROSSER
27397 Pte. H. BECKETT
34157 Sgt. H. MATHER
36965 H/C. H.R. WILBRAHAM

O.Davies
Lt Col
Commdg. 16th Bn R. Welsh Fus

Vol 35
113/38

16ᵗʰ R.W.T
WAR DIARY
FOR OCTOBER
1918

16TH (S) Batt. L.N. Fusiliers

Army Form C. 2118.

WAR DIARY
or
INTELLIGENCE SUMMARY.
(Erase heading not required.)

OCTOBER 1918.

Place	Date	Hour	Summary of Events and Information	Remarks and references to Appendices
Field.	1st		Battalion in Bivouac and Shelters near HEUDECOURT. Battn. H.Q. W.22.c.5.7; having carried out Battn. training and having Reinforcements - 89. O.Rs.	
	2nd			
	3rd		Battn. carrying out training. At 4.35 p.m. the Battn. less transport details proceeded by March Route to position in Railway cutting in front of PEZIERE (Companies occupied trenches in this Area.	
	4th		Moved off from above position 2.40 p.m. and proceeded to trenches near LEMPIRE (Tombois Farm)	
	5th		Spent the morning in position as above. Later moved to position near BASKET WOOD and LA TERRIÈRE, during afternoon. Casualties = 10 O.R. Killed.	
	6th		In above position. Casualties = 3 O.Rs Killed. 1 O.R. Wounded.	
	7th		After dark Battn. H.Qrs moved forward to new H.Qrs near MORTHO WOOD and Companies moved to probably positions. Reinforcements 2/Lt A.W. Clear	

Place	Date	Hour	Summary of Events and Information	Remarks and references to Appendices
Field	8th		Barrage opened 1.0 a.m. The Batt. attacked with "D" and "B" Companies in front, and "C" and "D" Companies in SUPPORT. At H.4 a.m. the 11th Infantry Brigade leap-frogged through to 115th Infantry Brigade.	
			Casualties — Officers — 2/Lt J.M. Davies — Killed. 2/Lt A. Paireyman — Wounded — Died of wounds 9/10/18. Capt. J. Fairclough MC — do — 2/Lt J.E. Hughes — do — 2/Lt T.B. Kennan — do — 2/Lt P.C. Harding — do — 2/Lt G.W. Carr — do — Lieut T.E. Evans MC — do —	
			O.R's. 34 O.R's — Killed 112 O.R's — Wounded 4 O.R's — Missing	
			During the afternoon proceeded to position near MALINCOURT dug in for the night. Reinforcements — 3 O.R's (Relief N.C.O's).	
	9th		In the afternoon Battalion moved into village and occupied billets there.	

Army Form C. 2118.

WAR DIARY
or
INTELLIGENCE SUMMARY.
(Erase heading not required.)

(3)

Place	Date	Hour	Summary of Events and Information	Remarks and references to Appendices
Field	10th 11th		Billets in MALINCOURT. Re-organization and refurnishing of Battalion.	
	12th		Battalion proceeded by cross country route practising Artillery formation and advance guards, to Billets in BERTRY.	
	to 19th		Training re carried out during stay in BERTRY Battle Surplus joined Battalion for training.	
	17th		Reinforcements — 94 O.R's.	
	19th		On the night 19/20th Battalion moves from BERTRY to Assembly positions H.Q.W. in bank near MONTAY. "C" Coy in CELLARS.	
	20th		Attack commenced 2.0 a.m. "A" and "B" Coys in FRONT. "C" and "D" Companies in SUPPORT. All objectives gained and consolidated.	
			Casualties — Officers — 2/Lt W. Young. M.C. Wounded	
			— 2/Lt A.W. Clear — do- absent	
			O.R's — 3 O.R's Killed.	
			— 19 O.R's Wounded	
			— 1 O.R. Missing	

Army Form C. 2118.

WAR DIARY
or
INTELLIGENCE SUMMARY.
(Erase heading not required.)

Instructions regarding War Diaries and Intelligence Summaries are contained in F.S. Regs., Part II. and the Staff Manual respectively. Title pages will be prepared in manuscript.

(4)

Place	Date	Hour	Summary of Events and Information	Remarks and references to Appendices
	21st		Battalion holding the line consolidated. Casualties — 1. O.R. Killed. 7. O.R's Wounded.	
	22nd		Reinforcements — 102 O.R's Battalion holding the line as on 21st. Casualties — 2. O.R's Killed. 5. O.R's Wounded. On the night of 22nd Battalion was relieved by a Unit of the 33rd Division, and Battalion was withdrawn to Billets in TROISVILLES. Reinforcement — 1. O.R.	
	23rd		Proceeded by march route to FOREST at 9.30 a.m. Casualties — 3. O.R's Wounded. Reinforcements — 1. Officer. Lt. Steadman.	
	24th 25th		Training and reorganization of Battalion. Casualties — Lt. H.L. Marsh — Wounded. — 1. O.R. NYD. Shell Shock.	
	26th		Battalion proceeded by Cross Country route in Artillery formation to position in front of VENDEGIES. Dug in	

Army Form C.2118.

Army Form C. 2118.

WAR DIARY
or
INTELLIGENCE SUMMARY.
(Erase heading not required.)

Place	Date	Hour	Summary of Events and Information	Remarks and references to Appendices
Sunk Rd near PAUL JACQUES FARM.	26th		Dug in Sunk Rd near PAUL JACQUES FARM. Reinforcements — 47 O.R's 1 Officer Capt C.J.S. Nicholls	
	30th		Training carried out by Battalion. Reinforcements — 44 O.R's	
	31st		42 O.R's	

Awards during the month.

Bar to M.C.
2/Lt. W. Young M.C.

M.C.
Capt. F. Mostyn.

Bar to M.M.
Pte. H. Bailiff
16022

Military Medal.

19529 Pte. W.J. Bradshaw 203827 Pte. S. Ingoill 247114 L/c J.S. Taylor
55788 " J. Thompson 368717 Sgt. J. Ellson 205286 Sgt. J.P. Beirne
73566 L/c B. Kennard 735428 " J. Humphries 235445 Pte J. Jones
55179 Cpl F. Bower 56550 L/c F. McDonald 58293 " J. Haycock
3747 L/c

M Dale Major.
for O.C. 16th R.W. Fusiliers

16th B.W.F.
War Diary
for
November 1918

NOVEMBER 1918.

Army Form C. 2118.

16TH (S) Batt. Royal Welsh
1154 Inf. Bde

WAR DIARY
or
INTELLIGENCE SUMMARY.
(Erase heading not required.)

Place	Date	Hour	Summary of Events and Information	Remarks and references to Appendices
Field	1st 2nd 3rd		Battalion in Area near Paul Jacques Farm. Casualties 1 O.R. Killed. 1 O.R. Wounded. Reinforcements – 1 O.R.	
	"		At night Bn Headquarters moved forward to ENGLEFONTAIN. Casualties – Killed 2 O.R's	
	4th		113th Brigade attacked 08.30. Heavy casualties in assembly positions. Very few casualties in the FOREST attacked. All objectives gained, 114th Brigade passed through 113th Brigade clearing. Battalion bivouaced in FOREST for the night. Casualties – OFFICERS – Wounded – 2Lt Gwilym Havard Rees. R.W. Rev. Hugh Evan Skyrme. L.L. (C.F.) O.Rs – Killed 23. Wounded 85.	
	5th		Moved forward at night. Bivouacked for night in Forest near LOCQUIGNOL. Reinforcements 10 O.Rs.	
	6th		Moved from above position about 14.30 and marched to BERLAIMONT. Battalion located in Billets	
	7th		Moved from BERLAIMONT 0.900 hours by march route to	

WAR DIARY or INTELLIGENCE SUMMARY.

Army Form C. 2118.

Place	Date	Hour	Summary of Events and Information	Remarks and references to Appendices
AULNOYE	7/11		Moved off from AULNOYE about 16.30 hours. Relieved 33rd Division in the line in Forest de Mormal (eastern edge of wood)	
			Reinforcements — Officers	
			Lieut. Walker Daglish Howick. MC	
			2/Lt. John Edward Jones	
			" Edward Davies	
			" Gwyneth Robert Owen	
			" John Thraves Goddard	
	8th		Battalion attacked 07.00. "A" Coy on left, "D" Coy in support. "C" Coy on left, "B" Coy on right, "D" Coy in Right. "C" Coy ordered forward to reinforce "B" Coy who were subjected to heavy M.G. fire. Objective line of road through W.26 central gained. Heavy shelling around Batt. H.Q. who were stationed on the edge of wood. At 12.00. Barrage crept forward from Road already occupied. Battalion advanced which "C" Coy on right followed by "D" Company on left followed by "A" Company. Objective gained, and Batt. H.Qrs moved forward to 13c. Battalion remained in above position the rest of the day. 15th Division moved forward through 16th Division in the evening	
			Casualties — Killed — 3 O.R's.	
			Wounded — 23 O.R's.	
			Missing — 2 O.R's.	

Army Form C. 2118.

WAR DIARY
or
INTELLIGENCE SUMMARY.
(Erase heading not required.)

(3)

Place	Date	Hour	Summary of Events and Information	Remarks and references to Appendices
Guise	9th		Morning devoted to cleaning up. Moved off the cross country route 15.30 hrs to DINECHAUX. Battalion billeted there. Bicycles supplied and sent on by "B" Coy	
	10th		Day devoted to cleaning up refitting and reorganising.	
	11th		Location of billeties 11.00 hrs. Battn. parade to convey news to the men. Bicycles supplied as yesterday. Reinforcements— 56 O.R's	
	12th 13th 14th 15th		Battalion training in DINECHAUX Area. Reinforcements Officers 1/Lt Austin Newbold Griffiths 2/Lt Arthur Mostyn Scott " F. A. Goord " R. E. A. Morgan O.R's 35.	
	16th		Battalion moved by march route OBRECHIES.	
	17th 18th		Training carried out.	

Army Form C. 2118.

WAR DIARY
or
INTELLIGENCE SUMMARY.
(Erase heading not required.)

(4)

Place	Date	Hour	Summary of Events and Information	Remarks and references to Appendices
Fleas	18th		Reinforcements - 23 O.R's	
	19th		Inspection of Battalion by Brigadier General H.E. ap Rhys Pryce C.M.G., D.S.O.	
	20th		Battalion Parade 0.9.45 Inspection by Brigadier General A. Carton de Wiatt. V.C., C.M.G., D.S.O. Reinforcements - Lieut John Malcolm Attwool. M.C.	
	21st		Brigade Parade on Brigade Ground at WATTIGNIES to VICTORIA Presentation of Medal Ribbons by the Divisional Commander.	
	22nd		Training carried out	
	23rd		Battalion route marched to SARBARA Reinforcements - Officers - Wilfred Stanley Brocklehurst 24 O.R's.	
	26th/27th		Training carried out Reinforcements - 27 O.R's	
			-do- OFFICER - Lieut David John Everall.	
	30th		Lieut Col C.E. Davies, D.S.O. left Battn to command 1st Inf Bde wea. Brigadier General A. Carton de Wiatt. V.C., C.M.G., D.S.O. to Division. Command of Battalion devolved upon Capt Wilfred Stanley Brocklehurst.	

WAR DIARY
or
INTELLIGENCE SUMMARY.

Army Form C. 2118.

Awards during November 1918

Bar to Military Cross
Capt. Acting Lieut. T.F. Evans. M.C.

Military Cross
Lieut. 2/Lt. T. B. Kenan
 "   "   A. C. Harding
 "   "   A. W. Clear

Distinguished Conduct Medal.
70524. L/Sgt. J. Ashcroft.
26691. Sgt.   F. R. Skraggon
93825. Sgt.   W. J. Howard.
203328. A/c.   R. Mowbray
19606. Sgt.   H. W. Chaplain. MM (att. T. 16 Battery)

Military Medal.
203328. A/c. R. Mowbray.
78161.   Pte. A. P. Evans.

Mardlyn
Lieut. Colonel
p.tt. Commanding 16th Brigade R.F.A.

16/17 R.W.F.

VII 37

WAR DIARY FOR DECEMBER 1918

37F

Army Form C. 2118.

WAR DIARY
or
INTELLIGENCE SUMMARY.
(Erase heading not required.)

16th (S) Bn R.W. Fusiliers
113th Inf. Bde
38th (Welsh) Division

DECEMBER 1918.

Place	Date	Hour	Summary of Events and Information	Remarks and references to Appendices
	1918. Dec. 1		Battalion occupying Billets in SARBARAS.	
	2/4		Training carried out during the morning, and recreational training in the afternoon.	
	3rd		In accordance with Bde March Table the Battalion proceeded to PETIT MAUBEUGE. The Bde was drawn up in Mass, and at 11hrs His Majesty The King passed along the road. Marched back to Billets.	
			Reinforcements — 2/Lt Leonard Evan Thomas. " Phillip Williams. " John Alexander Roberts. " Christopher Smeeting. " Vincent Coppack " Jot Thomas Davies 22 Other Ranks.	
	4.5. 6th		Carried out training.	
	24th		Christmas Dinner under Coy arrangements.	
	25th			
	26th		Training under Coy arrangements. 14th Reinforcements 76 O.Rs. 23rd " 8 " " "	

2.

WAR DIARY
or
INTELLIGENCE SUMMARY
(Erase heading not required.)

Army Form C. 2118.

Place	Date	Hour	Summary of Events and Information	Remarks and references to Appendices
	1918 Dec. 27th		Battalion proceeded by march route in accordance with Bde March Table, to Billets in HECQ.	
	28th		Marched from HECQ to Billets in INCHY.	
	29th		Entrained at 08.00 hrs and at 08.30 hrs the Brigade group moved off. Arrived WARLOY 16.00 hrs. Proceeded to CAMP just outside the village.	
	30/31st		Carried out training.	

AWARDS DURING MONTH.

M.C.   2/Lt. (A/Capt) F.R.Warren, M.M.

M.M.

2/Lt. J.L. Ralph.

28807 Cpl. D. Jones   54035 Pte. E. Tucker
54600 Pte. L. Jones   56483 L/C. O.J.Jones.
51613 Cpl. H. Johnson   26994 Pte. C. Frederick
40148 Pte. E. Vaughn   54494 Lge. F. Ashworth
15306 Pte. S. Wells   55372 Pte. E. Lee
27887 L/C. F. Brassett   18239 Pte. D.J. Jones

Army Form C. 2118.

WAR DIARY
or
INTELLIGENCE SUMMARY.
(Erase heading not required.)

Place	Date	Hour	Summary of Events and Information	Remarks and references to Appendices
	1918.		Mentioned in Despatches. Lt. Col. C. E. Davies, DSO. 19060 Sgt. H. Roberts.	

M Dale Major,
Commanding 16th Bn R.W. Fusrs.

16th Bn. Royal Welsh Fusiliers 9838

War Diary

for

January – 1919.

WAR DIARY or INTELLIGENCE SUMMARY

Army Form C. 2118.

16th (S) Batt. ROYAL WELSH FUSILIERS

Month of JANUARY 1919

Page 1.

Place	Date	Hour	Summary of Events and Information	Remarks and references to Appendices
Field	Jan 1st to Jan 31st		Training and Fatigues	
"	Jan 2		DEMOBILIZATION	
			REINFORCEMENTS.	
			Capt. Jacquier.	
"	4		4 men.	
"	5		15 men. 4 men	
"	6		3 men	
"	8		6 men	
"	11		Lt Reginald Chas. Rose Shopland	
			2/Lt Frank Arthur Goard	
			8 men	
"	12		12 men	
"	13		19 men	
"	14		Lt Benjamin John Stedman	
			7 men	
			Capt Jacquier	
"	15		12 men	14 men.

Page 111

WAR DIARY
16th (S) Batt Royal Welsh Fusiliers
INTELLIGENCE SUMMARY

Army Form C. 2118.

Month of January 1919

Place	Date	Hour	Summary of Events and Information	Remarks and references to Appendices
Field	Jan 1st		Award of D.S.O. to Major J.R. Dale M.C.	
"	" 16		Party consisting of Commanding Officer, Second in Command, the Adjutant and five other Officers together with sixteen O.R's. proceeded to ALLONVILLE for the presentation of the King's Colour.	
"	" 17		Battalion route marched to LONGUEVILLE station.	
Field	18th		Ceremonial Drill with the King's Colour.	

F. Dale Maj Jr.
Lieut. Col. Commanding
16th (S) Batt Royal Welsh Fus.

WAR DIARY or INTELLIGENCE SUMMARY.

Army Form C. 2118.

16(S.B) Batt ROYAL WELSH FUSILIERS

Month of JANUARY 1919

Place	Date	Hour	Summary of Events and Information	Remarks and references to Appendices
Field	Jan 18		DEMOBILIZATION	
"	19		7 men.	REINFORCEMENTS
"	20		2/Lt John Alexander Roberts 10 men.	5 men.
"	21		9 men.	
"	22		19 men.	
"	25		2/Lt Leonard Evan Thomas 12 men.	
"	26		12 men.	3 men.
"	27		12 men.	2 men.
"	28		12 men.	
"	29		12 men.	

Sheet 1 16th R.W. Fusiliers Army Form C. 2118.

WAR DIARY
INTELLIGENCE SUMMARY.
(Erase heading not required.)

February 1919

Place	Date	Hour	Summary of Events and Information	Remarks and references to Appendices
Worloy-Baillon	Feb 1st to Feb 28th		Training and Fatigues	
	Feby 2nd		Reinforcements	
	3rd			
	5th		Demobilization	
	6th		16 Other Ranks	
	7th		8 " "	
	8th		8 " "	
	9th		20 " "	
	10th		12 " "	
	12th		3 Other Ranks	
	13th		2 Lieut Christopher Sweeting and 11 ORs.	
	14th		2 Lieut Douglas Graham How and 9 ORs.	
	15th		Lieut. O.S. Lloyd Jones and 13 ORs.	
	16th		6 Other Ranks	
	19th		2 " "	
	21		5 " "	
	22nd		Major J.R. Dale, DSO, MC and 3 ORs	
			3 Other Ranks	

Sheet II
Army Form C. 2118.
16th R.W. Fusiliers

WAR DIARY
or
INTELLIGENCE SUMMARY.
(Erase heading not required.)

February 1919.

Place	Date	Hour	Summary of Events and Information	Remarks and references to Appendices
Warloy-Baillon	Feby 3rd	20.5	Demobilization 18 Other Ranks	
do	Feby 12th		" 9 "	
			The Battalion was re-organized into 2 Companies: men who were selected for the Cadre and men who were eligible for Demobilization were posted to 'B' Coy. The remainder who were for the Army of Occupation were posted to 'C' Coy.	
do	Feby 16th		Lieut John Malcolm Attwooll, M.C. proceeded to join 26th R.W. Fus.	
			2/Lieut Vincent Coppock " "	
			2/Lieut Arthur Leonard Evans " "	
do	Feby 20th		2/Lieut John Thraves Goddard and 50 Other Ranks proceeded to join the 26th R.W. Fusiliers at DUNKIRK	
do	Feby 6th		H.R.H. The Prince of Wales paid an informal visit to the Camp.	

O.D Harris Lt Col
16 R.W.F

Sheet 1.

WAR DIARY
INTELLIGENCE SUMMARY

16th Batt Royal Walsh Fusiliers

March 1919

Army Form C. 2118.

Place	Date	Hour	Summary of Events and Information	Remarks and references to Appendices
Warloy Baillon	March 1st-16th		Training and fatigues carried out.	
do	March		A draft of the 5 undermentioned officers and 20 Other Ranks proceeded to join the 26th Bn R.W.F.	
			Lieut J.B. Warren, M.C., M.M.	
			Lieut R.A. Jones	
			Lieut T.B. Price, M.C.	
			Lieut J.L. Ralph, M.C.	
			2/Lieut F. Thompson, D.C.M.	
do	March 17th		The undermentioned Regular Officers proceeded to the United Kingdom and were posted to the Depot, Wrexham.	
			Lieut A.N. Griffiths	
			2/Lieut E.W. Gillia, M.M.	
do	March 19th		The Battalion proceeded by march route to the hutted camp near the village of Blangy-Tronville	
Blangy-Tronville	March 19th-31st		Training and fatigues carried out.	

Sheet II

Army Form C. 2118.

WAR DIARY
or 16th (S) Batt Royal Welsh Fusiliers
INTELLIGENCE SUMMARY.
(Erase heading not required.) March 1919

Place	Date	Hour	Summary of Events and Information	Remarks and references to Appendices
Blangy-Tronville			Awards	
			Star of Roumania - Officers 6 Lieut Col. E.E. Davies, D.S.O.	
			Demobilization	
	Mar 1st		5 Other Ranks	
	5th		9 " "	
	7th		3 " "	
	8th		3 " "	
	13th		6 " "	
	15th		5 " "	
	19th		4 " "	
	26th		1 " "	

W.P. Boekelwort Captain
Commanding 16th Batt. R.W. Fusrs

WAR DIARY or INTELLIGENCE SUMMARY

16th (S) Batt Royal Walsh Regt
Army Form C/2118
Month of April 1919

Vol 41

Place	Date	Hour	Summary of Events and Information	Remarks and references to Appendices
Blangy-Tronville	Apl 1st-30th		Training and fatigue carried out.	
do	Apl 2nd		Lt. Col. E. E. Davies D.S.O. proceeded to the 53rd Batt. Royal Warwick Regt. and the command of the Battalion was taken over by Capt Wilfred Stanley Brocklehurst.	
do	Apl 9th		The Battalion took part in a Route March by the 38th Division Infantry Cadres, to St. Nicholas (Amiens sheet 1/100000 2 E 82) and back	
do	Apl 14th		The Battalion took part in a Route March by the 38th Division Infantry Cadres to Villers Bretonneux (Amiens sheet 1/100000 2 G 25) and back	
			Demobilisation	
do	Apl 6th		Capt. J. Fairclough. M.C. and 4 Other Ranks	
do	Apl 13th		4 Other Ranks	
do	Apl 20th		2/Lieut A. M. Scott, 2/Lt. J. T. Davies and 1 Other Rank	
do	Apl 27th		Lieut E. Thomas and 2 Other Ranks	

(Brocklehurst)
Capt. a/y
16th Batt R.W. Regt m.g.

www.ingramcontent.com/pod-product-compliance
Lightning Source LLC
Chambersburg PA
CBHW080850230426
43662CB00013B/2067